D0394658

The Penguin Book of
# Canadian Biography
# for Young Readers
# Volume II, 1867–1945

The Penguin Book of
# Canadian Biography
# for Young Readers
# Volume II, 1867–1945

Barbara Hehner

PUFFIN
CANADA

PUFFIN CANADA
Published by the Penguin Group
Penguin Books, a division of Pearson Canada, 10 Alcorn Avenue, Toronto, Ontario, Canada M4V 3B2
Penguin Books Ltd, 80 Strand, London WC2R 0RL, England
Penguin Putnam Inc., 375 Hudson Street, New York, New York 10014, U.S.A.
Penguin Books Australia Ltd, 250 Camberwell Road, Camberwell, Victoria 3124, Australia
Penguin Books India (P) Ltd, 11, Community Centre, Panchsheel Park, New Delhi – 110 017, India
Penguin Books (NZ) Ltd, cnr Rosedale and Airborne Roads, Albany, Auckland 1310, New Zealand
Penguin Books (South Africa) (Pty) Ltd, 24 Sturdee Avenue, Rosebank 2196, South Africa

Penguin Books Ltd, Registered Offices: 80 Strand, London WC2R 0RL, England

First published 2002

1 3 5 7 9 10 8 6 4 2

See page 267 for photo credits.

Front cover photo credits: (clockwise from upper left): E. Pauline Johnson (Portrait Gallery of
Canada, C-085125); Nellie McClung (Portrait Gallery of Canada, PA-030212); Stephen Leacock
(Portrait Gallery of Canada, C-085125); Elsie MacGill (Portrait Gallery of Canada, PA-200745);
John Ware (Glenbow Archives, NA-263-1); Frederick Banting (Portrait Gallery of Canada,
PA-123481); Billy Bishop (Portrait Gallery of Canada, PA-001654); Sir Wilfrid Laurier
(National Archives of Canada, C-4960); Sam Steele (Portrait Gallery of Canada, PA-028146).

Back cover images (clockwise from upper left): Lester Patrick (Hockey Hall of Fame);
E. Cora Hind (Glenbow Archives, NA-1451-10).

Front flap image: Archibald Belaney, a.k.a. "Grey Owl" (Portrait Gallery of Canada, PA-122479).

Printed and bound in Canada on acid-free paper ∞

NATIONAL LIBRARY OF CANADA CATALOGUING IN PUBLICATION DATA

Hehner, Barbara
The Penguin book of Canadian biography for young readers : 1867–1945,
volume II / Barbara Hehner.

Includes index.
ISBN 0-14-301346-7

1. Canada—Biography—Juvenile literature. I. Title.
II. Title: Canadian biography for young readers : 1867–1945.

FC25.H44 2002      j971'.009'9      C2002-903968-1
F1005.H44 2002

Visit Penguin Books' website at **www.penguin.ca**

*To Eric—This book is yours as much as mine*

# Contents

Acknowledgements x

Introduction xi

Donald Smith (Lord Strathcona) 1

Sandford Fleming 7

Timothy Eaton 13

Hannah Maynard 18

Anderson Ruffin Abbott 23

Wilfrid Laurler 28

Henri Bourassa 34

John Ware 40

Alexander Graham Bell 44

Sam Steele 49

Joseph-Elzéar Bernier 55

Robert Borden 60

Ned Hanlan 66

Kit Coleman 71

Adelaide Hunter Hoodless 75

Joseph Burr Tyrrell 79

E. Cora Hind 84

E. Pauline Johnson 89

James Naismith 94

Martha Black 99

Reginald Fessenden 103

Maude Abbott 108

Stephen Leacock 114

R.B. Bennett 119

Emily Carr 125

Sam McLaughlin 131

Nellie McClung 136

William Lyon Mackenzie King 142

Lucy Maud Montgomery 150

Tom Thomson 155

Arthur Currie 160

John McCrae 166

Billy Bishop 171

J.S. Woodsworth 176

Robert Boyd Russell 182

Angus Walters 189

Lester and Frank Patrick 195

Tom Longboat 200

Archibald Stansfeld Belaney ("Grey Owl") 206

Norman Bethune 212

Agnes Macphail                                          218

Frederick Banting                                       223

Wilfrid Reid "Wop" May                                  228

Lionel Conacher                                         233

Howie Morenz                                            238

Bobbie Rosenfeld                                        243

Lucien Dumais                                           248

Elizabeth Gregory "Elsie" MacGill                       253

Andrew Mynarski                                         258

The Dionne Quintuplets                                  262

Photo Credits                                           267

Index                                                   269

# Acknowledgements

F IRST OF ALL, thank you to Pat Hancock, for providing an excellent model with Volume I of *The Penguin Book of Canadian Biography for Young Readers.* Thank you to Barbara Berson of Penguin Books for matching me with this project, and to Diane Turbide and Joel Gladstone, also of Penguin, for shepherding it through editorial and production with professional skill and kindness. Dennis Mills, a longtime friend from the Editors' Association of Canada, proved to be a meticulous copy editor. Susan Wallace-Cox, Sandy Cooke, and Amanda McCormick of Pearson Canada found some wonderful photographs to illustrate the biographies. Thank you also to several people who helped me track down biographical information: Tanya Barbeau of Veterans Affairs Canada; Kristin Johannsdottir; Colin Macgregor Stevens; Pam Wakewich; and Allison Mailer, Brigette Bouchard, and Abigail DeLeong of the BC Sports Hall of Fame. Finally, my gratitude to my husband, Eric Zweig, for his enthusiasm for Canadian history and for his creative and editorial skills.

# Introduction

THE SPAN OF THIS BOOK—1867 to 1945—is just eighty years. That's about the length of a human life. Yet within that relatively brief period, Canada went through extraordinary changes.

In 1867, the year of Confederation, Canada had only four provinces and about three and a half million people. By 1945, Canada stretched from sea to sea and up to the Arctic Ocean. Newfoundland (which would join Canada in 1949) was the only missing province. The population had grown to twelve and a half million, swelled partly by millions of immigrants from the British Isles, from Northern and Eastern Europe, from the United States, and from many other parts of the world. During that span of years, the telephone, the automobile, and the airplane were invented. Canada fought in two terrible world wars, sacrificing over 100,000 of its people—mostly very young men—in the process.

In this book, you will find fifty Canadians who made their mark during those eighty years, although some were born before 1867, and many lived on after 1945. The oldest were born long before Confederation, when Canada was just a small string of British colonies along the border with the United

States. Two of them were still alive as I wrote the book—the remaining sisters of the Dionne Quintuplets.

It is fascinating to write fifty Canadian biographies at one time. There were recurring patterns in these people's lives, revealing ways that the country was growing and changing. Many of them, for instance, were born and raised on farms. At the time of Confederation, about eighty percent of Canadians lived in rural areas. Even as late as the 1930s, about a third of Canadians were still farming the land. (Today, under five percent do.) Many of the people in this book began life in Ontario, Quebec, or the Maritimes (the earliest areas of Canadian settlement) but moved west in adulthood, as the Western provinces joined Confederation and Western communities sprang up. Several went as far north as Yukon at the time of the Klondike gold rush.

Another clear pattern was that almost all the women in this book faced hurdles in gaining an education or pursuing a career because of prejudice. They were pioneers who made the path easier for women who came after them.

On the lighter side, I enjoyed noticing the odd connections between people. Reginald Fessenden designed the electrical lighting for the 1893 Columbian Exposition which so impressed reporter Kit Coleman, even though she probably never knew his name. Stephen Leacock and John McCrae, author of "In Flanders Fields," belonged to the same literary club in Montreal. Norman Bethune, who became a hero to the people of China, and Frederick Banting, who discovered insulin, were in the same class in medicine at the University of Toronto.

Where the connections between people were large and important, I have made a note in the biography to lead you from one to another. As you read, perhaps you will even find a family connection to one of these people, as I did. (Archie Belaney, the author better known as Grey Owl, turned out to have been in the same regiment as my grandfather during World War I.) Personal connection or not, all of these people had a hand in shaping the Canada that you live in today. I hope you will enjoy your journey through their lives.

# Donald Smith
## (Lord Strathcona)
### 1820–1914

ONALD SMITH is the central figure in a famous Canadian photograph known as "Driving the Last Spike." He is a spry-looking man of sixty-five, with a top hat and a fluffy snow-white beard. He is bent over, holding a tool called a spike maul, ready to hammer a spike into a railway line. Everyone else is watching him respectfully, because Donald Smith is one of the richest, most powerful men in the country. His energy and courage, combined with ambition and even ruthlessness, have taken him far from his humble beginnings.

Donald Alexander Smith was born on the coast of northern Scotland, in the town of Forres. His father could barely support the family on his income as a merchant. His mother had two brothers who had gone to Canada to work in the fur trade, and from an early age, young Donald was fascinated with the idea of the Canadian wilderness. However, his mother believed that such a life would be a waste of his good marks in school. So, when he graduated at sixteen, Donald Smith went to work in the town clerk's office in Forres to learn about the law. But his mind was far away, still focused on the vast Hudson's Bay Company territory known as Rupert's Land.

A few months before his eighteenth birthday, Smith travelled to London to meet his fur-trading uncle, John Stuart. He told his uncle that he wanted to go to Canada, and Stuart wrote him a letter of introduction to Sir George Simpson, governor of the Hudson's Bay Company. Smith sailed for Canada on May 16, 1838, and arrived in Quebec City on June 30. He quickly made his way to Montreal by steamship, then walked eight miles to the town of Lachine, where the Hudson's Bay Company had its headquarters. Governor Simpson read the letter from John Stuart and hired Smith as an apprentice clerk. The job paid £20 (less than $100) per year.

For the next three years, Smith worked in Lachine or at nearby trading posts, counting muskrat furs. He had not yet found the adventure he had been looking for, but he was at least learning the business of the fur trade. Smith became an excellent judge of the quality and value of the different furs and also came to understand how the various company accounts were managed. Then, in 1841, George Simpson assigned Smith to the trading post at Tadoussac, northeast of Quebec City. He spent the next six years at Tadoussac and at the even more remote post of Mingan.

Late in 1847 Donald Smith became worried about his health. He had begun to suffer from snow-blindness—a temporary loss of sight caused by the sun's glare off the snow. When he learned that he might become permanently blind, he wrote three letters to

Governor Simpson asking for permission to see a doctor in Montreal. After receiving no reply, he made the 1,900-kilometre trip on a sailing ship and walked into Simpson's Lachine mansion, unannounced, at dinner time. An angry Simpson agreed to let Smith be examined by his own personal physician. Then, when he was assured that Smith would not go blind, he banished him to one of the Hudson's Bay Company's bleakest outposts, at North-West River on the eastern shore of Labrador. Smith was given just half an hour to prepare to leave Montreal.

Because it was winter, there were no stage coaches running north out of Quebec City, so Smith had to walk hundreds of kilometres back to Mingan. He had hired two native guides to lead him through the wilderness, but one of them died along the route. At one point on the journey, their food supplies were so low that they had to eat moss boiled in a pot with the skin of a beaver. Smith finally reached Mingan in mid-January of 1848, then set out again for St. Augustine, 800 kilometres away. He was so exhausted by the time he got there, that he could not continue his journey until the spring.

In April, he and two more Indian guides paddled up the St. Augustine River, finally arriving at the trading post at the town of North-West River. Smith would live for years at this settlement and nearby Rigolet, and he became quite content with his life in Labrador. By 1853 he had taken over from Richard Hardistry as chief trader and had married Hardistry's daughter Isabella. Together, Smith and his wife established a small farm at North-West River. Despite the short growing season, the farm was quite successful and raised much of the food their family needed. Smith was also in favour of fishing and sealing off the coast of Labrador, so that when the fur trade began to decline, the Hudson's Bay Company continued making money from the sale of salmon and seal oil. This led to Smith's promotion to chief factor in 1862.

As Smith moved up the ranks of the company, he had to make frequent trips to Montreal. There, he met many influential business-men, including his cousin George Stephen. These men helped Smith invest his money wisely, and he had plenty of money to invest. Smith had not only his own savings, but also the savings of many of the Labrador traders who trusted him with their money. He gave the traders the profits they expected, but his own profits were enormous and he became a well-respected businessman in Montreal. Soon, he was living in the city full-time, after being appointed head of the Hudson's Bay Company's Montreal department.

In 1869 Donald Smith was put in charge of the company's western operations at their headquarters in Fort Garry (soon to be the city of Winnipeg). Smith arrived just as the company was getting ready to sell off its huge western territory to the Canadian government. The transfer of land was one grievance in the Métis rebellion, which Donald Smith would help to settle. In addition to his duties with the Hudson's Bay Company, Smith was appointed a special commissioner by Prime Minister Sir John A. Macdonald. Though he was held for three months as a prisoner by Louis Riel's provisional government, Smith helped bring about a peaceful solution, which cleared the way for the province of Manitoba to join Confederation in 1870.

That same year, Donald Smith was elected to represent the city of Winnipeg in the new Manitoba provincial legislature. One year later, he was elected to the House of Commons in Ottawa as the representative from Selkirk, Manitoba. Smith was elected as a Conservative, but in 1873, he turned against his leader, Sir John A. Macdonald, over an issue known as the Pacific Scandal. (Macdonald was said to have taken bribes from Sir Hugh Allan, head of the company that was slated to build the Canadian Pacific Railway.) Smith may have chosen not to support Macdonald because he wanted to be involved in the building of the railway himself.

During his time in Manitoba, Smith had become convinced of the importance of railways in building up Western Canada. By 1877 Smith and George Stephen had taken over a bankrupt American railway, the St. Paul and Pacific Railway, and extended it to the Manitoba–Minnesota border—and then they connected the line to a railway they had built south from Winnipeg. The success of this project brought them millions of dollars. By the time Smith left politics in 1880 (amid allegations he had bribed voters), he had helped put together a new Canadian Pacific Railway syndicate, with George Stephen as the president. Smith was one of the company's largest shareholders, but he kept his name in the background because Sir John A. Macdonald, who was prime minister again, was still very angry with him.

Preliminary work on the cross-Canada railway had begun under Sandford Fleming in 1871, but work had progressed slowly between 1874 and 1878, when Alexander Mackenzie was prime minister. The new CPR company promised Macdonald they would complete the railway by 1891, and they hired William Cornelius Van Horne to oversee construction. He pushed his workers hard, through difficult terrain, including the eastern forests, the mountains of the West, and the combination of rock and swamp around Lake Superior. The building of the railway was harder than anyone had predicted, and costs kept going up, but Donald Smith never lost faith. Both he and Stephen risked their entire fortunes, but still the syndicate had to borrow more and more money from the government.

By the time the last spike was driven, on November 7, 1885, the railway had cost more than $150 million. But it was worth it: the Canadian Pacific Railway would unite the country and ensure its growth. The railway's success would also make the men who built it even more wealthy than they had been.

Donald Smith was knighted by Queen Victoria in 1886, and the following year he returned to politics and represented the riding of Montreal West. Smith was seventy-six years old when he retired from the House of Commons in 1896. That year, he was offered the position of high commissioner (the equivalent of an ambassador) for Canada in England. In 1897 Smith was raised to the rank of British nobility, taking the title of Lord Strathcona.

Lord Strathcona spent the final seventeen years of his life living in London, but he worked hard in the interests of Canadian trade and immigration and made sure that Canada's opinions were heard at the centre of the British Empire. When the Boer War broke out in 1899, he financed his own Canadian mounted regiment, which was named Lord Strathcona's Horse. The regiment included many former members of the North-West Mounted Police and was commanded by Colonel Sam Steele. (For more about the regiment and the NWMP, see Sam Steele's biography.) Lord Strathcona's Horse helped establish Canada's reputation for bravery on the battlefield, an image that would grow during the First World War. Donald Smith died on January 21, 1914, just a few months before the outbreak of that war and just two months after the death of his beloved wife. He was ninety-three years old.

# Sandford Fleming
## 1827–1915

I N THE NINETEENTH CENTURY—long before the days of automobiles and airplanes—the invention of the steam engine and
railway trains began to "shrink" the world. Cross-country trips
that might have taken weeks or even months, by ship, on horseback,
or on foot, could now be completed in days, and in relative comfort,
too. But imagine trying to schedule train travel when every town
along the route had its own system of telling the time. In each
community, clocks were set to reach noon when the sun passed
directly overhead. This meant that when it was noon in Kingston,
Ontario, it was already twelve minutes past twelve o'clock in
Montreal, and it was still thirteen minutes before noon in Toronto.

In the days before high-speed travel, locally based times had not presented much of a problem. By the middle of nineteenth century, however, passengers on a train would have to reset their watch at every stop along the way. Many travellers carried more than one watch, or used watches with six different dials on the face. Obviously something had to be done. The man who solved the problem, by developing the concept of Standard Time, was Sandford Fleming. He was also the man responsible for building many of Canada's most important railways. And to help streamline yet another form of travel—the delivery of mail—he designed Canada's first postage stamp.

Sandford Fleming was born in Scotland but came to Canada shortly after his eighteenth birthday, in 1845. Sandford and his older brother, David, made their way to Peterborough, in Canada West (now Ontario), where a relative, Dr. Hutchison, was working. The brothers spent the summer with him, then travelled to Toronto in search of jobs. David found one almost immediately, but Sandford had a more difficult time. He had been trained as a surveyor in Scotland, and hoped to find engineering work in Canada. Fleming carried with him letters of introduction to several prominent builders, but the important men he met in Toronto seemed to believe there was nothing more in Canada that needed to be built—despite the fact that only sixteen miles of railway existed in the entire country.

Discouraged, Fleming returned to Peterborough, where Dr. Hutchison was able to find him a job with a government surveyor. The government man measured and mapped the country around them, while Fleming did the drawings that put the plans on paper. Soon, he was making his own maps of towns like Peterborough, Newcastle, and Cobourg. By 1847 both Fleming brothers were doing so well for themselves that they encouraged their parents and the rest of the family to emigrate from Scotland to Canada. The family settled just west of Toronto, where they operated a mill on the Humber River. Meanwhile, Sandford Fleming travelled the countryside east of Toronto, selling his maps and the drawings he made of interesting buildings he saw along his tour. In 1849 he went to Montreal to take the formal examinations for his licence as an official land surveyor.

Fleming returned to Toronto after obtaining his licence and rented an office on Yonge Street. He spent most of his first two years in business drawing up plans for the Toronto harbour and designing schools. Like most businessmen in the days before the invention of the telephone, Fleming relied on the mail to conduct his business. However, he quickly grew tired of standing in line to have each of his letters individually rated. England had begun using postage stamps in 1840, and the United States adopted the practice in 1847. On February 24, 1851, Fleming met with Postmaster-General James Morris to discuss the possibility of producing stamps. His design, known as the Three-Penny Beaver, became Canada's first postage stamp. It was also the first time that the beaver was used, officially, as a national symbol.

A year after the issue of his postage stamp, Sandford Fleming embarked on the job that would change his life. In 1852 he was hired as one of two assistant engineers on a new railway called the Ontario, Simcoe and Huron. The line was to be built from Toronto to Barrie, and then on to Collingwood. Over the next eight years, Fleming spent much of his time wandering through the wilderness, surveying the land over which the railway would be built. Accurate measurements were a must. He also produced detailed sketches for the construction of bridges, and he became skilled at the scientific use of the materials needed to build these bridges. Fleming was appointed chief engineer of the project in 1855. That same year, he married Jean Hall of Peterborough.

The Ontario, Simcoe and Huron Railway was completed in 1860—just in time for a ride by the Prince of Wales. The future King Edward VII was in Canada to tour the country on behalf of his mother, Queen Victoria. The Prince rode the train with Fleming from Toronto to Collingwood, and the two men got along well. Nearly forty years later, in 1897, the Prince's mother would knight Sandford Fleming for his invention of Standard Time.

In 1863 Sandford Fleming was thirty-six years old. His work— and his wise investments—already meant he would never have to worry about money again, but there was much he still hoped to accomplish. He proposed a plan to build a railway right across Canada, but the colonial government (Canada was still four years away from Confederation) was not yet ready for such an ambitious project. In the meantime, Fleming was named chief surveyor of the Intercolonial Railway, which would link Quebec City to Saint John, New Brunswick, and Halifax, Nova Scotia. By 1868 surveying was completed and construction had begun, with Fleming serving as engineer-in-chief. Railway bridges had traditionally been made of wood, but Fleming insisted that iron and stone bridges would be safer and last longer.

Construction of the Intercolonial Railway was not yet complete when the Canadian government named Sandford Fleming chief engineer of the Canadian Pacific Railway project in 1871. He hired a team of surveyors to help him find the best route from Quebec and Ontario to British Columbia. Conditions in the uncharted Canadian West were not only rough but extremely dangerous. A team of twelve surveyors drowned one summer, while another group of sixteen men were killed in a forest fire. Eventually, Fleming found what he thought was the safest route through the Prairies and across the Rocky Mountains. At first the government supported his idea, but then plans were changed to take a more southern route. (Later, other railways would follow

Fleming's path.) When the government decided to turn over the CPR to a private company in 1880, Fleming retired from the project. He would be on hand, however, when Donald Smith drove "the Last Spike" on November 7, 1885. (See the biography of Donald Smith for more about this.)

Between 1880 and 1885, Sandford Fleming had devoted much of his time to the issue of . . . time. Britain and France already had standardized times for train travel, but North America did not. Fleming, however, wanted more than just a North American system; he wanted a system for standardizing time around the world. Fleming first wrote a paper on the subject in 1879. He also devised a world map, which he divided into twenty-four time zones, based on the lines of longitude. There would be a one-hour difference between adjoining time zones, but all the clocks within one zone would always indicate the same time. Fleming's idea was both simple and practical, yet it was rejected for years by governments and scientific societies. Some people even argued that standardized time was contrary to the will of God.

Finally, Canada and the railways in North America adopted Sandford Fleming's concept of Standard Time in 1883. Then, in October 1884, an international conference was held in Washington. The result of the International Prime Meridian Conference was that on January 1, 1885, Standard Time was scheduled to take effect everywhere. In actual fact, it took a few years longer, but by the end of the nineteenth century, Standard Time had come into force around the world.

The last of Sir Sandford Fleming's great technological achievements would take even longer than Standard Time to become reality. As early as 1879, Fleming had proposed that a telegraph line should be run along the floor of the Pacific Ocean, to link Canada and Australia. A similar cable under the Atlantic Ocean already linked Canada and England, yet few people seemed to take Fleming's idea of a Pacific cable seriously. The idea, however, was proven to be financially sound in 1894, and by 1897, public opinion across the British Empire was in favour of the cable. Plans eventually got under way in 1899, and the cable was ready for use on October 31, 1902. The first message transmitted was a greeting to King Edward VII from the British colony of Fiji. The first message to Canada came from the prime minister of New Zealand, congratulating Sir Sandford Fleming. Few men had done as much as he had to make Canada and the world ready for the twentieth century. He passed away in Halifax in 1915 at the age of eighty-eight.

# Timothy Eaton
## 1834–1907

TIMOTHY EATON was born in County Antrim in the north of Ireland. He was the youngest child in a prosperous farming family. His father died two months before he was born, but his mother, with the help of her older children—there were nine in all—continued to manage the farm. Then a great disaster struck Ireland, changing the course of life in that country and in North America. Potatoes were the staple crop of Ireland. But in 1846 a blight caused the potato crop became black, mushy, and inedible. The same thing happened the following year. For many Irish, the choices were cruel and simple—starve to death or leave Ireland. Thousands of desperate men, women, and children crossed the ocean to North America.

The Eatons' plight was not as dire as that of many others, but the farm could no longer support all the children. Two brothers (and later three sisters) emigrated to Canada. Meanwhile, still in Ireland at the age of fourteen, Timothy became an apprentice to a shopkeeper in Portglenone, a town near his home. His employer sold a wide array of goods, including clothing, cattle feed, groceries, liquor, and medicines. Timothy often worked from four in the morning until midnight, and he was always exhausted. To snatch a little more sleep, he would sometimes curl up under the shop counter at night instead of going home. Hard as the work was, though, he was learning a great deal about how to stock a store and how to run it.

As soon as the five years of his apprenticeship were over, Timothy Eaton boarded a ship for Canada. He had a new suit of clothes and £100 in his pocket (equal to about $12,000 today). At first he worked on his sister's farm near Georgetown, Ontario, but he soon got a job working as clerk and bookkeeper in a general store.

In 1860 he and his two older brothers opened a store that sold dry goods (fabric and clothing) and groceries in the Ontario town of St. Mary's. Here, to Eaton's growing dissatisfaction, business was still done in the traditional way, with no fixed prices. Hours were spent in haggling (bargaining with customers over the price of items) and bartering (accepting, for example, a farmer's chickens or sacks of wheat as payment for a bolt of cloth). Eaton wanted his own business, which he could run according to his own ideas. Encouraged by his wife, Margaret, whom he had met at church in St. Mary's, he decided to open a store in Toronto. The Eatons, along with their three children, moved to the bustling city of 70,000 people, twenty times the size of St. Mary's.

On a freezing cold December 8 in 1869, T. Eaton Co. Limited opened for business in a small shop at 178 Yonge Street. There were three employees, plus Eaton himself, to serve the customers they hoped would arrive. Eaton had run an advertisement in the Toronto *Globe* with a statement that raised eyebrows: "We propose to sell our goods for CASH only—in selling goods we have only one price." There would be no bargaining over the prices; and all customers, no matter how humble, would be treated equally. To sweeten this new way of selling, Eaton made another pledge: "Goods satisfactory or money refunded." Torontonians flocked to the store.

Eaton was soon in competition with another merchant—the Scottish immigrant Robert Simpson, who had opened a nearby store similar to Eaton's. In 1883 Eaton made sure that he kept his customers by opening a new, much larger store farther north on Yonge Street. It was like nothing Toronto had ever seen: a department store with four shopping floors reached by two elevators. The store also featured electric lighting and ladies' restrooms. Soon there would be escalators, and stylish red-and-black delivery wagons, with uniformed drivers and well-groomed horses, to bring purchases right to customers' homes. But it was another innovation that changed the company from just a store into a beloved Canadian institution.

In 1884 the T. Eaton Company published a mail-order catalogue so that customers, anywhere in Canada, could order goods from the store. The first Eaton's catalogue was a simple price list, thirty-two pages long, with no pictures. But by the early 1900s, the catalogue was a thick, illustrated volume. Some people called it "the wishing book." Out West, it was known as "the Prairie Bible." Rural Canadians, with no stores nearby, especially looked forward to the arrival of the catalogue. Many evenings were spent studying its pages, checking off items, and writing orders. When the new catalogue arrived, children often asked for the old one. They could cut out paper dolls from the ladies' fashion pages, and young hockey players could use the thick books as shin pads. And finally, tattered catalogues might end up in the outhouse as toilet paper.

The T. Eaton Company kept pace with people's needs. There were different editions of the catalogue for various regions of the country. The catalogue for the Prairies concentrated on supplies needed by pioneering families. In 1898, during the Klondike gold rush, the catalogue offered a complete set of clothing and equipment for someone heading to the goldfields. Eventually, the Eaton's mail-order department occupied three buildings and had its own printing press.

Timothy Eaton was, for his day, an enlightened employer. Remembering the exhausting hours he had once put in as a store clerk, he closed his original store at eight in the evening, two hours earlier than other stores. In 1880 he moved the closing time to six o'clock. He also closed his stores on Saturday afternoons in July and August, so that his staff could have some recreation time. He liked to think of himself as a father to his employees, keeping track of all their names and the names of their children, and taking care of those who were sick or needy. But he was a morally strict father. He did not believe in frivolity, including smoking, drinking, and card playing. One hundred years after the first store opened, Eaton still did not sell tobacco products or playing cards. He also detested labour unions. One employee later claimed, perhaps exaggerating a little, that Timothy Eaton would fire anyone who looked out the store's windows at a Labour Day parade.

Eaton's only hobby outside of work was his stable of carriage horses. When he was in his late sixties, he was thrown from his carriage and badly injured his hip. But he lived long enough to see his son, John Craig Eaton, open a new, five-storey department store in Winnipeg. Sitting in his wheelchair, Eaton held his grandson Timothy, who was two years old, while the boy pushed a bell that opened the doors of the store. When Timothy Eaton died of pneumonia in 1907, the T. Eaton Company had its own factories to supply the stores with merchandise, offices in London and Paris, and 9,000 employees.

# Hannah Maynard
## 1834–1918

I N THE LATE 1970S, a young researcher looking through picture files in the British Columbia Archives came upon a very
odd photograph. At first glance it was just a photograph of
two proper women, dressed in the style of the 1880s, having a
prim little tea party. However, when the researcher looked more
closely, she saw that both the ladies having tea appeared to be
the same woman. A portrait hanging on the wall behind them
showed yet another identical woman. Oddest of all, she was leaning out of the picture frame and pouring tea from her china cup
onto one of the tea drinker's heads. The picture's label said that it
had been taken by Hannah Maynard. The researcher soon learned

that the strange photograph was a self-portrait. And it turned out that there were boxes and boxes of negatives and prints in the archives, unseen for many decades, all taken by the same eccentric photographer.

Hannah Hatherly was born in Cornwall, England. When she was eighteen, she married Richard Maynard, an apprentice bootmaker. Together they sailed to Canada and settled in Bowmanville, a town in Canada West (later Ontario). For a while they lived a settled life. Richard opened a boot-making shop, and Hannah gave birth to three children. Then, in 1858, Richard headed for British Columbia, where gold had been discovered. Unlike so many others who sought riches around the Fraser River, he actually found gold—not enough to become hugely wealthy, but enough to live a very comfortable life. When he returned to Bowmanville, he found that Hannah had also been busy. She had been studying to become a professional photographer.

In the 1850s, photography was a recent invention, and cameras were large and bulky. There were no cameras for home use; anyone who wanted a picture taken had to go to a photographer's studio. The exposure times for early film were very long: in fact, the subjects had to hold their position for such a long time that clamps were used to hold their heads still. No wonder people in nineteenth-century photographs often look so stiff and uncomfortable! Years later, one of the children Hannah Maynard photographed remembered the strain of the occasion: "There was Mama, keeping a firm grip on Simon's shoulder so that he would not move. . . . And just look at Samantha, practically weeping, because she had to stand on that poor dead polar bear! Mrs. Maynard was almost hidden by black cloth, working behind the huge black box, the camera. Just a few more minutes . . . everyone still! There!"

The Maynards decided that there was more opportunity for them out West, so they packed up and journeyed to Victoria,

British Columbia. When Hannah arrived with her family, in 1862, she found a town of "tents, gullies, and swamps." Richard soon left to do more prospecting for gold, and Hannah opened a photography studio in the family home on Johnson Street. Nearly everyone in the rough, unfinished town of Victoria had come from somewhere else and wanted a picture to send back home. Hannah Maynard's studio was soon bustling and successful. When Richard returned this time, he found that Hannah's business was well established. He opened a boot-making shop next door, and he also began to take photography lessons from his wife.

Richard preferred photographing scenery. On his many restless journeys around the province, he took pictures of mountains, icebergs, gold-rush towns, and the construction of the CPR. As the years went by, he was accompanied by his eldest son, Albert. Hannah went on some of these journeys, and also travelled alone to the Queen Charlotte Islands. But her real love was photographing people. She was fascinated by faces.

Hannah moved her studio to a bigger, finer, brick building. Victoria was growing into a prosperous, sophisticated city and Hannah's business grew with it. Eventually, she could claim, without much exaggeration, that she had photographed every resident of Victoria at least once—often as babies. After about twenty years of portrait making, Hannah began to create more unusual pictures. She created collages of all the babies—hundreds of them— that she had photographed in a year. Hannah called the collages "Gems of British Columbia." The "Gems" began as a yearly promotional piece for her photography studio, to be mailed to friends and customers. Each tiny baby photo was reduced to small size, cut out, placed on a background, and then the whole arrangement was rephotographed. Over the years, the "Gems" became more and more elaborate: the children were arranged to form a fountain, a cross, interlocking diamonds. In 1891 the centre collage of babies and children was framed by smaller squares that repeated the "Gems" from eleven earlier years. With a magnifying glass, it would be possible to see about 22,000 faces in this one.

At the time, people were charmed by the "Gems," which were reprinted in newspapers as a popular annual feature. But there is sadness behind some of them, too. Mixed in with the living children are images that appear to be small white statues. They may be memorials to the child that Hannah lost: her beautiful daughter Lillie, who had often modelled for her mother's camera, died in 1883 at the age of sixteen.

Hannah found solace in her work, which was becoming more and more inventive. To create the illusion of a statue, she would completely cover someone with white powder before he or she posed. To create just a head or a bust, she would block out the rest of the sitter with black cloth, then combine the image with a pedestal. She called this effect "living statuary."

Even more adventurous were the multiple images she began to experiment with. Each one posed technical problems that Hannah clearly enjoyed solving. She could make "twins" of a subject by covering the left half of the camera lens and photographing a person on the side that could be seen; then she would cover the right half of the lens cap, move the person to the other side, and make a second exposure on the same plate as the first. Other pictures were made by blacking out areas of the photographic plate itself, or by using mirrors to create multiple reflections. Some of the finished photographs are unsettling to look at. In one, two ladies (both Hannah) and a young boy, Hannah's grandson, gaze at a piece of frozen white "living statuary," which is clearly also her grandson. In another, a whole roomful of Hannahs socialize with one another. The long exposure times required would not allow Hannah to photograph motion: however, she created the illusion by posing people on bicycles as if they were riding, with hidden braces holding the bicycles upright and still.

Hannah continued to make beautiful portraits in her studio, using delicate and flattering lighting, which she devised herself. For a portrait of her granddaughter, taken around 1900, she painstakingly embossed parts of the image, working from the back with a paper knife. The puffed fabric of Laura Lillian's sleeves, her nose, the curls in her hair, are all rounded on the front of the picture. Such work is so difficult to do without tearing the picture that there are very few examples of this technique.

Richard Maynard died in 1907. Hannah retired from photography in 1912, and died in 1918 at the age of eighty-four. Her pictures were largely forgotten until researcher Claire Weissman Wilks rediscovered them and wrote a book about Hannah Maynard's work. Today, Hannah Maynard's genius is widely recognized. Her original vision and technical skill produced photographs that were decades ahead of their time.

# Anderson Ruffin Abbott

## 1837–1913

I N 1861 a terrible war in which more than 600,000 people would die began in the United States. It pitted the northern half of the country against the southern half, and one of the main issues of the war was slavery. The agricultural wealth of the South had been built on the labour of black slaves. When the government of the United States moved to abolish slavery, the southern states withdrew from the Union. Soon the divided nation was at war.

Canada—still just a string of British colonies along the northern American border—watched anxiously. At least 50,000 Canadians served in the Civil War, most on the Union side. These men (and a handful of women who served in male disguise) must have had many different reasons for joining the fight. However, a large number were from American families that had resettled in Canada. Black Canadian settlers felt an especially strong call to join the fight against slavery. One of these was a remarkable doctor named Anderson Ruffin Abbott.

Abbott was born in Toronto, the third child in a large family. His parents had been "free persons of colour" who left the United States because of the racism they encountered there. Abbott's father had to abandon a successful business when the family left Mobile, Alabama. However, he prospered again in Toronto as a real-estate broker. Abbott received an excellent education, partly at the Buxton School in the new black settlement of Elgin, near Chatham. Many of the students of this school went on to higher education, including Abbott, who entered the University of Toronto. He graduated with a degree in medicine at the age of twenty-three. In 1861 the Medical Board of Upper Canada granted him a licence to practise medicine. He was the first Canadian-born black medical doctor.

However, there was a black doctor already in practice in Toronto, who became Abbott's mentor. His name was Alexander T. Augusta, and he was originally from Virginia. He was a few years older than Abbott, in charge of the Toronto City Hospital. When the Civil War broke out, Augusta returned to the United States to see what he could do to help.

Although many Northerners wanted to abolish slavery, and were willing to go to war over it, even in the North there was widespread prejudice against African Americans. More than a year passed before the American Congress finally allowed black men to fight for the Union. They were organized into sixteen Colored (then an acceptable term used by both black and white people) Regiments, separate from white soldiers. Seventy young men from the small Elgin settlement where Abbot had gone to school hurried to enlist in Detroit, Michigan. For black doctors, the wait was even longer.

Doctors were always given officer's rank, but racist factions in the army did not want to give commissions (appointments as officers) to African Americans. In the spring of 1863, Augusta finally became a major and surgeon-in-charge of the Seventh United States Colored Troops at Camp Barker Hospital in Washington, D.C. He was the first African American to head a hospital in the United States.

Abbott was still in Toronto, but eager to join Augusta. In February 1863, he had written a letter to the U.S. Secretary of War, which began, "I learn by our city papers that it is the intention of the United States to raise 150,000 colored troops. Being one of that class of persons, I beg to apply for a commission as Assistant Surgeon." He went on to lay out his excellent medical qualifications. But his letter was not answered. He tried again in April, giving Augusta as a reference. Finally, in June, he received the appointment he had sought. He became an assistant surgeon to the United States Army with the rank of captain. Of the 11,000 surgeons who cared for the Union Army during the Civil War, only eight were African Americans.

Abbott became part of the bloodiest war in U.S. history. Weapons of war were more accurate and more destructive than they had ever been, but medical treatment lagged behind. Field hospitals often lacked such basics as clean water to wash hands and instruments, and most wounds became infected. In the time before antibiotics, infected limbs had to be amputated to save the patients' lives. More arms and legs were removed by surgeons during the Civil War than at any time, before or since, in American history. But wounds weren't the only hazard of military hospitals. Crowded together, men easily caught pneumonia, typhoid fever, and dysentery. Even childhood diseases such as measles and chickenpox could be deadly for already weakened men.

By the standards of the day, Abbott, who was better trained than many other Civil War surgeons, had excellent working conditions. He joined a well-staffed and well-equipped hospital for black soldiers near Washington, D.C. At first he was supervised by Augusta, but he later took charge. Among his patients was a corporal who turned out to be a young black woman in disguise. Although Abbott discovered her true identity, she convinced him that she could continue to carry off her deception and serve the army well. Abbott treated her and allowed her to return to her regiment without giving away her secret.

Sometime during the winter of 1863–64, Abbott and Augusta were invited to a levee (reception) at the White House. At this large gathering, in their full-dress uniforms, they received many curious stares. They were the only African Americans in the room. (Abbott wrote later that he supposed they may have been the first black men ever to attend a White House levee.) However, President Abraham Lincoln greeted them warmly. It was the beginning of a friendship that lasted until the president was assassinated in April 1865. In memory of that friendship, the president's widow, Mary Lincoln, later gave Abbott a shawl that had belonged to Lincoln.

In 1866 Abbott returned to Canada, and after spending a few years as a physician in Toronto, he became the county coroner in Chatham, Ontario. In 1871 he married Mary Casey of St. Catharines, Ontario, and eventually they had seven children. His busy activity in community affairs included the presidency of the Wilberforce Educational Institute, a school that prepared students of all races for university.

In 1894 Abbott became the medical superintendent of Provident Hospital and Training School in Chicago. This hospital had been founded to give black doctors and nurses, shut out of other hospitals by racism, a place to practise medicine. However, white doctors and nurses were also employed there, and patients of all races were accepted. He and his wife retired to Toronto in 1897, living comfortably on inherited wealth from Abbott's father. With more leisure in his later years, Anderson Abbott wrote many newspaper articles that spoke out against racial discrimination. He died in Toronto at the age of seventy-six.

# Wilfrid Laurier
## 1841–1919

SIR WILFRID LAURIER was prime minister of Canada from 1896 until 1911. He was the first French Canadian to lead the country. Others have held the office for more years in total, but no one else has been prime minister for so many consecutive years. Laurier was a handsome and stylish man, who always wore a diamond horseshoe pin in his cravat for good luck. He was a successful leader who believed in the basic goodness of ordinary people. He believed that the weak had to be protected against the strong and powerful. His respect for people and their different points of view made him able to reach compromises, and his ability to compromise helped him balance the beliefs of

French and English Canadians. Better relations between the two main language groups were at the heart of everything Laurier tried to do.

Four years before Wilfrid Laurier was born, there had been an uprising in what would become the province of Quebec. When the British army defeated the French-Canadian rebels, known as the Patriotes, some of the fighters were executed. Many others were sent to dungeon-like prisons. Growing up when he did, Wilfrid Laurier saw evidence that direct attacks against the English would only make things worse for the French. The two groups of people would have to work together and understand each other in order to make Canada strong. Laurier's father believed this, too. When young Wilfrid was ten (his mother had died when he was seven), his father sent him to live with an English family in New Glasgow, Canada East (later Quebec). Although this town was just 11 kilometres from St. Lin, where Laurier was born, he could learn to speak English there. Perhaps even more importantly, he also found out that people of different backgrounds could come to appreciate each other.

When Laurier was thirteen, he was sent to a Roman Catholic school, the main purpose of which was to train boys to become priests. But when he was twenty, Laurier chose to study law at Montreal's McGill University. He was now just over six feet tall, but frail and sickly. He would battle bronchitis for his whole life. Still, in 1864 he graduated near the top of his class and became a lawyer in Montreal.

Two years later, Laurier became sick and left Montreal for the small town of Victoriaville, where the cleaner air might improve his health. He became the editor of a newspaper called *Le Défricheur*, but it soon went out of business and he went back to practising law. In 1868, he married Zoe Lafontaine, a piano teacher. However, it is Emilie Lavergne who deserves credit for turning the young country lawyer into a polished gentleman. She was the wife of Laurier's law partner, and they would remain friends for years.

Although the Montreal law office he had worked in was headed by a prominent Liberal and Le Défricheur was a Liberal newspaper, Laurier did not run for office until 1871. He was elected to the Quebec Assembly that year, resigned in 1874, and was then elected to the House of Commons in Ottawa. The Liberals lost the next election in 1878, but Laurier managed to keep his own seat. However, his party would be in opposition for the next eighteen years, while the Conservatives formed the government.

Laurier was not well known outside of Quebec until 1885. Sir John A. Macdonald's Conservative government had been ignoring calls for help from the Métis and other native peoples in the West, and soon their peaceful struggle became a rebellion. The government finally responded by sending out soldiers and arresting Louis Riel, the Métis leader. The Métis were Catholic and spoke French, and Laurier was sympathetic to their cause. So were the people of Quebec. But the rest of Canada was against Riel. Laurier had to find a way to support the Métis leader without angering the rest of the country. He did this by blaming the Conservatives for the trouble, saying that there never would have been a rebellion if Macdonald's government had been fair to the Métis in the first place. Laurier's speech about the Métis proved popular with Liberals across the country, and in 1887 he became leader of the party. Still, the Liberals lost the next election, in 1891. Soon, though, Laurier had to deal with another issue.

French Catholics in Manitoba had always enjoyed French-language schools in their education system. In 1890 the provincial government stopped paying for these schools, which angered Quebec. The Canadian government tried to force Manitoba to continue operating the schools, which angered Ontario. The case eventually went to court, but the issue still had not been settled when a federal election was called in the spring of 1896. Laurier promised that, if the Liberals were elected, he would settle the Manitoba Schools Question with a "sunny ways" approach. By this he meant that he would use gentle persuasion instead of imposing his political power. The Liberals won the election, and Prime Minister Laurier settled the dispute with a compromise— there would no longer be French-only schools in Manitoba, but French would still be used in schools where enough French-speaking students warranted it. Most people were pleased with the resolution of the problem.

In 1897 Laurier and his wife travelled to England to represent Canada in festivities to mark Queen Victoria's sixtieth year on the throne. As a French-speaking person who had become the leader of England's oldest colony, Laurier attracted a great deal of attention. He was asked to give many speeches and was chosen to ride directly behind the Queen in the Diamond Jubilee Parade. He also received a knighthood from the Queen, making him Sir Wilfrid Laurier.

In return for the attention lavished upon him, British politicians hoped that Laurier would strengthen the ties between Canada and England. Laurier actually believed in greater independence for Canada, but he knew it was important (especially in Ontario) that Canada show its support for the British Empire. Without giving any real commitments, he promised that Canada would always do what it could to help Britain. It was not long until his attachment to the Empire was tested.

In 1899 Britain went to war against the Boers (Dutch settlers) in South Africa. Canada was expected to join the war effort. Ontario, in particular, was willing to demonstrate its support of the Empire, but Quebec was not. Quebeckers felt sympathy towards the Boers and thought Canada should not get involved in a British war. Again, Laurier was forced to compromise. Canada would send a volunteer army to South Africa, but Britain would pay for it. Not everyone was happy with the plan, but the majority of people accepted it.

Though issues with Britain took up much of Laurier's time, his biggest concerns were with Canada itself. Laurier's government worked very hard to attract new immigrants to the wheat fields of the Canadian Prairies. Clifford Sifton, the minister of the interior, enticed people from the United States and Europe to the "Last Best West." New settlers poured in; new railways were built across the country; and Canadian wheat was sold around the world. Canada was growing so quickly that soon Laurier could declare in a speech, "I think we can claim that Canada will fill the twentieth century." He could also promise that, if re-elected, he would create two new provinces in the West. The Liberals easily won the election of 1904, and Alberta and Saskatchewan entered Confederation in 1905.

Canada's population was increasing and the economy was booming, but not all was well. Quebec leaders like Henri Bourassa worried that a growing Canada was becoming less and less French. (For more about his views, see the Henri Bourassa biography.) Then, in 1909, a new issue began to threaten French-English relations. Germany had begun to build up its navy, so Britain appealed to all its colonies to make contributions to strengthen the Royal Navy. With Bourassa leading the way, Quebec argued that Canada should be independent and that giving money to the British Navy could drag the country into another war. English Canada, on the other hand, demanded that the money be paid. In 1910 Laurier reached a compromise—Canada would create its own navy, which could be loaned to England if there was a war. This time, though, no one was happy.

To relax after the stress of the naval debate, Laurier took a trip across Western Canada during the summer of 1910. While he was there he heard farmers complaining about tariffs. Tariffs made goods from outside Canada cost more than those made inside the country. Laurier decided to remove the tariffs and negotiate Reciprocity (free trade) between Canada and the United States. It turned out, though, that most Canadians were against free trade. They were afraid that a trade deal would give the United States too much influence over Canada. In the general election of 1911, even some farmers voted against the Liberals. Quebeckers who were still angry about the navy issue turned away from the Liberals, too. Laurier's government was defeated by the Conservatives.

Laurier was now seventy years old and had been in public office for forty years. But he believed he still had a role to play in soothing English–French relations, and he stayed on as leader of the Liberals. He kept his popularity within the Liberal Party until the First World War.

When the fighting started in 1914, most Canadians supported the war effort, but soon there were not enough volunteers. In 1917 Prime Minister Borden introduced Conscription—a plan to draft men between the ages of twenty and forty-five into the army. Quebeckers were outraged that British interests were being put ahead of Canada's. Laurier had never believed in forcing people to do things, but many Liberals agreed with Conscription. To Laurier's sorrow, they left him to join Borden's Union govern-ment, which easily won the next election, in December 1917. When Conscription was introduced in 1918, just as Laurier had feared, there were protest riots in Quebec.

By the time the First World War ended on November 11, 1918, Laurier was once again being recognized as a great Canadian. After his death on February 17, 1919, some 50,000 people lined the streets of Ottawa as his funeral procession passed. Hundreds of dignitaries from across the country were on hand. Two eulogies were delivered—one in French and one in English.

# Henri Bourassa
## 1868–1952

H ENRI BOURASSA was just three years old when his grandfather, Louis-Joseph Papineau, died, but Bourassa would remember him always. Papineau had led the Rebellion of 1837, which saw French Canadians rise up to oppose the injustices of the small British clique that governed Quebec (then called Lower Canada). Like his grandfather, Henri Bourassa would come to inspire the people of his province. He believed that Quebec had an important role to play in the country, because he believed in a strong Canada, with equality for both the French and English languages and cultures. This was the principle on which the country had been founded in

1867, and Bourassa would defend the rights of French Canadians whenever he felt they were being neglected.

Henri's mother was the daughter of Louis-Joseph Papineau, but she died when Henri was just six months old. He and his brother and sister were raised by their father, Napoléon Bourassa—a painter and novelist—and their mother's sister, Ezilda Papineau. The family lived in Montreal, but spent their summers on the Papineau estate in Montebello, a village on the Quebec side of the Ottawa River. The estate, which had belonged to Bourassa's grandfather, had been in the family since 1801.

The estate at Montebello was a holdover from the old seigneurial system. In fact, when Henri Bourassa inherited the estate in 1887, there were still many settlers there who would now lease their land from him. He spent a great deal of time getting to know these local people and became so popular that he was elected mayor of Montebello in 1890. He was just twenty-two years old at the time. A new federal riding called Labelle was created around Montebello in 1892, and soon there were rumours that Bourassa would be running for Parliament.

Bourassa had first been attracted to politics in 1885. That year, the execution of Louis Riel, who had led the Métis in their fight for rights in Western Canada, had become the most important French-Canadian issue since the Rebellion of 1837. Bourassa was inspired by the words of Wilfrid Laurier, who felt the best way to prevent injustices like those against Riel and the Métis was through hard work in Parliament. Laurier had become leader of the Liberal Party by 1896, and he asked Bourassa to run as the Liberal candidate in Labelle in that year's election. Bourassa agreed, but he had two conditions. One was that he would not accept financial support from the party. This would help him with his second condition, which was that he be free to reach his own decisions on issues—even if they went against what the party wanted.

Bourassa's political style was very different from that of Wilfrid Laurier. Both supported the view that Canada should seek more independence from England, but as prime minister, Laurier had to be concerned with balancing all points of view. Bourassa could afford to be much more outspoken. When Britain supported the United States over Canada in the Alaska Boundary Dispute of 1896, Bourassa was outraged. He believed the decision proved that Canada could not depend on Britain for support. When Britain asked Canada to help fight in the Boer War in South Africa in 1899, Bourassa was against it. He believed Canada should not have to fight for British imperialism, particularly in a war that did not threaten Canadian security. Laurier tended to agree, but English-speaking Canadians wanted the country to show its support for England. (For more about the issues that divided Laurier and Bourassa, see the Wilfrid Laurier biography.)

With pressure coming mostly from Ontario, Laurier decided that Canada would send a volunteer army to fight in South Africa. The compromise would allow those who believed in supporting England to join up, but would not force anyone who was opposed to the war to do so. Still, Bourassa was angry enough to quit the Liberal Party. The people of Labelle voted him back into office as an Independent candidate in 1900. After that election, Bourassa would generally support the Liberal point of view, but not always.

During the next few years, Bourassa fought Laurier over the Liberal government's immigration policy. With his minister of the interior Clifford Sifton leading the way, Laurier's Liberals were filling Western Canada with new settlers. Many came from the United States and England, but people also came from other

European countries. Very few immigrants spoke French. Bourassa felt it was in the best interest of Canadian unity for there to be more French Canadians in the Prairie provinces. He was concerned that French Canadians were becoming a smaller and smaller percentage of the country's entire population. Back in 1896, he had helped Laurier reach a compromise solution when French education was threatened during the Manitoba Schools Question. Now he was disappointed to see the new provinces of Alberta and Saskatchewan (created in 1905) establish English-only schools.

By 1908 Bourassa had left federal politics for Quebec provincial politics, but soon a major issue brought him back to the national scene. For several years, England had been asking Canada to provide money to help strengthen the Royal Navy. Germany was building up its own navy, and as the German threat increased, many English Canadians wanted Laurier's government to donate money so England could build three new Dreadnought battleships. Laurier knew that French Canadians did not support this view, and again he tried to reach a compromise. In 1910 he proposed that Canada create its own navy, which could be loaned to England during times of war. Bourassa attacked Laurier's proposal in the brand-new newspaper, *Le Devoir*, which he had founded. As he had during the Boer War, Bourassa argued that Laurier's policy would drag Canada into wars that did not threaten the country's safety.

Bourassa also disagreed with the Liberals over the issue of Reciprocity (free trade) with the United States. As a result, he gave his support to the Conservative Party in the election of 1911. Robert Borden became the new prime minister, but Bourassa would not support him for long. He had hoped Borden would halt the plans for a Canadian navy, but in 1912 Borden proposed sending $35 million to England to build battleships. In the end, the money was never sent, but Bourassa now found himself attacking the Conservatives just as hard as he had fought the Liberal Party. The biggest fight was yet to come.

The First World War began in the summer of 1914. As a British colony, Canada was at war as soon as England declared war on Germany on August 4. At first, the entire country was behind the war effort. Canadians from east to west volunteered for the army in great numbers. Even Bourassa wrote, in *Le Devoir*, that it was "Canada's national duty to contribute." He encouraged the recruitment of an entirely French-Canadian regiment, the Royal Vingt-Deuxième (Royal 22nd), who would become the famous "Van-Doos."

As the war dragged on, volunteer enlistment dwindled and Borden's government began to talk about Conscription—a draft of men between the ages of twenty and forty-five. English Canadians agreed. French Canadians did not. "Canada has already raised an army of 420,000 men from a population of 7 million," Bourassa argued. "This is equivalent to an army of 2.4 million for France, 2.7 million for England and 6 million for the United States. . . . To ask Canada to do more is an outrage."

In order to make Conscription the law, Borden's Conservatives joined with Liberals who supported his view to form a Union government. (For more about this, see the Robert Borden biography.) Bourassa now returned his support to Laurier and what remained of the Liberal Party, but the Union government won a huge victory in the election of 1917. Though his cousin Talbot Papineau, a captain in the Canadian Army, was angered by Bourassa's views, Bourassa continued to speak out against Conscription. Many blamed him when anti-Conscription riots broke out in Quebec City in April 1918.

Bourassa now began to look less at politics and focus more of his attention on work for the Catholic Church. This work increased after the First World War ended in November 1918, and continued following the death of his wife in January of 1919 and the death of Wilfrid Laurier one month later. Bourassa finally ran for election again in the riding of Labelle in 1925. He stepped down as director of *Le Devoir* in 1932, then retired from politics after his defeat in the election of 1935.

Just as Bourassa was leaving the political arena, Maurice Duplessis was coming to power in Quebec. Duplessis headed up a new party called the Union Nationale, which encouraged French Canadians to take a more active role in the financial affairs of Quebec, where most companies were run by English Canadians. Bourassa supported many of the party's views but worried that the Union Nationale was more interested in leading Quebec towards independence from Canada than preserving French rights within Canada. Still, when Conscription became an issue again during the Second World War, Bourassa came out of retirement to fight for the views of his province.

Now in his seventies, Henri Bourassa suffered a severe heart attack in 1944. He was not expected to survive, and though he did, this time he went into complete retirement. He died eight years later, on the eve of his eighty-fourth birthday.

# John Ware
## 1845–1905

J OHN WARE WAS BORN on a plantation in South Carolina, the second youngest of eleven children. Until African American slaves were freed by President Abraham Lincoln's Emancipation Proclamation in 1863, John Ware legally belonged to his master. He was never given the opportunity to learn to read and write; and he later said that he had never even worn a pair of shoes until he was twenty years old. However, Ware was not unskilled. He combined great strength—he was more than six feet tall and weighed about 200 pounds—with outstanding riding ability. After the Civil War—the war that ended slavery in the United States—Ware went West to look for work as a cowboy.

In the late nineteenth century, some 35,000 cowboys worked on vast cattle ranches in the American West, and about one in five of them was an African American. Cowboys kept watch over the herds and drove them hundreds of kilometres to railheads where they could be sold. It was hard, dusty work, and cowboys were in the saddle from dawn to dusk. But for Ware and many other black men, the cowboy's life brought a chance to earn fair wages. Furthermore, when they met racism out West, they could often overcome it by displaying skills that other men had to respect.

In 1882 John Ware joined a 700-mile (about 1,100-km) cattle drive heading from Idaho to a ranch in the Rocky Mountain foothills, southeast of Calgary. The drive had been organized by Tom Lynch, who was taking 3,000 head of cattle north to start a ranch in what would later become the province of Alberta. Ware was assigned to "the drag end," the muddiest, smelliest position behind the herd. And the horse he was given was a worn-out nag. However, by the time the cattle reached their destination, Ware was riding in front of the herd, on a very handsome, spirited stallion.

It happened this way. Ware had asked for a better mount, and Lynch, assuming Ware knew little about horses, had given him a wild-eyed, unbroken animal that was considered unrideable. The cowboys gathered around, expecting to see Ware thrown into the dirt. However, Ware soon brought the bucking bronco under control. Lynch was so impressed that when the herd reached the Bar U Ranch, he asked John Ware to stay on.

Ware accepted, and he worked at the Bar U for several years. Then he took an unusual assignment at the Quorn Ranch in Sheep Creek. It had been founded by a British fox-hunting club to breed horses that would be shipped to England—both for hunting and for British cavalry regiments. John Ware had full responsibility for the animals. It was on the Quorn Ranch that Ware became recognized as one of the most extraordinary horsemen in the Canadian West. In June 1885, the Macleod *Gazette* reported, "The horse is not running on the prairie which John cannot ride, sitting with his face either to the head or tail, and even if the animal chooses to stand on its head or lie on its back, John always appears on top when the horse gets up, and smiles as if he enjoyed it—and he probably does."

All this time, Ware had been slowly building up his own herd of cattle; sometimes he would take animals in lieu of wages. In 1890, Ware started his own small ranch near Sheep Creek. His cattle were branded 999, his lucky number.

Around the same time, Ware met Mildred Lewis, daughter of a homesteading family recently arrived from Toronto. Their courtship got off to a memorable start. Ware took Mildred on a buggy ride into the countryside. A sudden fierce storm came up, and lightning struck right beside the buggy. The couple was unharmed but their two horses fell down dead, still in harness. Ware hauled the buggy back to the Lewis home himself. In 1892 he and Mildred were married and moved into a log house beside Sheep Creek. They began to raise a family, which eventually grew to five children.

In 1892 ranchers in the Calgary area staged what they called a "gymkhana"—it would be called a rodeo today. Some 200 people attended a day of racing, bronco riding, and other "western" events. The star of the day was John Ware, demonstrating steer-wrestling (also known as bull-dogging). No one had ever seen a man wrestle a longhorn to the ground bare-handed, by gripping its horns and pulling it down. Ware had been invited to demonstrate this dangerous activity after some cowboys had seen him wrestle a steer to keep it from charging a group of men working in a corral. By the summer of 1893, it was part of the rodeo's schedule, with three men competing. The prize was a hand-made saddle—and John Ware won it.

John Ware's fame spread all over the West, and he seemed larger than life. Stories were told about his courage, agility, and strength: how he could run across the backs of cattle in a pen; how he could leap into the saddle without touching the stirrups; and how he could lift an eighteen-month-old steer to throw it on its back for branding.

By 1900 John Ware had 300 head of cattle, and he needed more grazing land than he could get near Sheep Creek. So he sold his ranch for $1,000 and the Ware family moved north, to land on the Red Deer River, near the village of Duchess. Here the Ware herd grew to 1,000 head.

In the spring of 1905 an unseasonable blizzard struck. Mildred Ware became ill with pneumonia, and before her husband could fight his way through the storm to get medical help for her, she died. Their five children went to stay with their Lewis grandparents, while a grieving John Ware worked the ranch. Then, just a few months after his wife's death, John Ware, too, died in a freak accident. His horse tripped on a badger hole and fell on him. His funeral in Calgary was the largest the young city had ever seen. The Wares' second log house, relocated to Dinosaur Park in the Alberta Badlands, is now restored and run as a museum to this remarkable man.

# Alexander Graham Bell
## 1847–1922

OST CANADIANS consider Alexander Graham Bell one of their own, although Bell was not a Canadian citizen. From his early twenties onward, his ties to Canada were strong, and some of his most impressive achievements occurred in Brantford, Ontario, and Baddeck, Nova Scotia.

Alexander Bell (he later added the "Graham" himself, in honour of a family friend) was born in Edinburgh, Scotland. He was the second of three boys in a creative family. His mother was an artist and, although an impairment kept her from hearing her own playing, an accomplished pianist. His father had wanted to be an actor, but this was not considered a respectable occupation at the time. Instead, he gave lessons to students who wanted to become effective public speakers. Alexander was a curious, creative, and inventive child. Like his parents, he was interested in art and poetry, but he also loved science. He collected and classified animal bones, and observed the stars. He figured out a way to communicate with his deaf mother—by speaking close to her forehead so that she could feel the changing vibrations made by his voice.

Alexander also took a great interest in his father's invention of "Visible Speech." This was a set of written symbols that stood for the way the throat, tongue, and lips should move to make all the different sounds of language. The senior Bell used his system to help his speech students, but Alexander had other ideas for its use. He and his older brother built a mechanical dummy with a tin throat and a wooden, cloth-covered tongue, as well as bellows for lungs. Working together to make these parts move, they created human-like sounds. By holding and moving the family dog's muzzle and throat while it barked, Alexander also got his good-natured pet to "speak" a few simple words, like "mama."

The Bells' happy life in Scotland ended when Alexander was just past twenty. His younger brother, only eighteen, and then his older brother, age twenty-five, died of tuberculosis within three years of each other. Alexander himself was showing symptoms of lung disease. His parents had heard that the crisp, clean air of Canada was far healthier than the polluted city air of Edinburgh. In 1870 the remaining family of three boarded a steamer for Canada. Soon they were settled in a pleasant house overlooking the Grand River, near Brantford, Ontario. Here, Alexander Bell recovered rapidly.

In 1871 Bell's father was invited to demonstrate Visible Speech at a school for the deaf in Boston, Massachusetts. He was too busy to go, so he sent his son instead. The school was impressed with the younger Bell and hired him to use Visible Speech to teach their students to speak. Soon, Alexander Bell was teaching courses to hearing-impaired students all over New England. In 1872 he set up a school in Boston where other teachers could learn his methods by watching him teach. One of Bell's most famous students was Helen Keller, who came to him as a child unable to hear, see, or speak. Another of his students, Mabel Hubbard, became his wife in 1876. By then, he was hard at work on his most famous invention.

Since childhood, Bell had been interested in the vibrations of speech. Now he raced against other inventors to perfect a device that he first called "the harmonic telegraph." The original telegraph had been around since the 1840s, but it could send only a series of beeps—the long and short tones of Morse Code. However, Bell devised a way to send the vibrations of the human voice through a wire, using an electrical current that varied in strength according to the different tones produced by the speaker. In March 1876, in his workshop in Boston, Bell transmitted his voice to his assistant in the next room. This was the world's first telephone call. Bell quickly patented his invention, which would make him rich and famous, and he founded the Bell Telephone Company. He was twenty-nine years old.

In the summer of 1876, at his parents' Brantford home, Bell continued his experiments. Using an existing telegraph line, Bell set up a long-distance call on the evening of August 10. In Brantford, Bell's uncle read from *Macbeth*, and his father recited from *Hamlet*. Both were heard clearly by an excited Bell on a telephone receiver set up in the Paris telegraph office, 13 kilometres away. The first two-way, long-distance call took place in October of that year, between Cambridgeport and Boston (just over 3 kilometres apart).

In the summer of 1885, Alexander Bell's family, which now included two little girls, Elsie May and Daisy, first visited Cape Breton Island. In 1892 the Bells built a grand mansion at Baddeck, on Cape Breton, where the rugged landscape reminded Bell of Scotland. For the next thirty years the Bells would spend the summer months there. In the laboratories and workshops on the spacious grounds of his house, Bell worked at his scientific research, and he hired local people to work as his assistants. He developed a version of the phonograph; an electrical instrument for surgery that could locate metal fragments in bullet wounds; and a device that carried sound, over a short distance, on a beam of light. By the 1890s, however, Bell's main interest had become the challenge of flight.

He began experimenting with propellers and kites. He built large tetrahedral kites—a tetrahedron is a form with four triangular faces—whose shape provided a great deal of surface area to catch the wind, but with little weight. In 1907 one of his kites had lifted a man 50 metres into the air. Bell decided he was ready to move on to experiments with heavier-than-air vehicles.

In September of 1907, Bell formed the Aerial Experimental Association. Among the other members were Glenn Curtiss, who had just started to design motors for flying machines, and J.A.D. McCurdy, a recent University of Toronto graduate from a prominent Baddeck family. The team began working on a biplane made of steel tubing, wire, and wood, covered with rubber-coated silk that was manufactured for balloons. This vehicle had a rudder but no brakes. After constructing a few test models, the men built a plane called the *Silver Dart* for the silvery colour of its fabric. On February 23, 1909, J.A.D. McCurdy, twenty-three years old, piloted the *Silver Dart* above the ice of Baddeck Bay—the first controlled, powered flight in Canada and the British Empire.

Bell also worked on designing boats that could use air to lift them out of the water. By 1908 he and F.W. (Casey) Baldwin—an engineering friend of McCurdy's—had built a model hydrofoil. In 1919 one of the hydrofoils Bell developed travelled 114 kilometres per hour over a 1.6-kilometre water course, a world record that stood for ten years.

Alexander Graham Bell remained active and enthusiastic into old age. He told a reporter a few months before his death, "There cannot be mental atrophy in any person who continues to observe, to remember what he observes, and to seek answers for the unceasing hows and whys about things." When Bell died at the age of seventy-five, all telephone service in North America was shut down for a minute in tribute to him.

# Sam Steele
## 1849–1919

THE UPRIGHT AND HONEST Canadian Mountie, doing good for the good of the country, is a familiar fictional character. But the true tale of Sam Steele of the North-West Mounted Police is more amazing than any writer or film-maker would invent. It seemed that wherever trouble appeared in Canada during his lifetime, Sam Steele was there to uphold the law. When Fenian raiders attacked Canada from the United States, Sam Steele was there. When the Métis rebelled in Manitoba and Saskatchewan, he was there. He was in Alberta and British Columbia when railway workers required protection. When order needed to be brought to the Klondike after the gold rush, the Canadian government turned to Sam Steele. When Canadian soldiers fought in the Boer War, he was there. He was there, again, when the troops marched off to battle in the First World War—even though by then he was sixty-five years old!

Though he would become the most famous lawman in the Canadian West, Sam Steele was born in Orillia, Ontario. His father had been an officer in England's Royal Navy, and Sam grew up on stories of dedication and duty. He was a fine student in school, but received an even greater education in the outdoors. "In those days," he would later write, "every man and boy—and many girls and women—could shoot [a rifle], and all men and boys could ride [a horse] well. I had the benefit of all this." These skills would serve him admirably throughout his life.

Sam Steele was just seventeen years old when the Fenians attacked Canada from the United States in 1866. The Fenians were a secret revolutionary society that fought to win Ireland's freedom from British rule. Irish-American Fenians attempted to support the cause by taking over Canada. Steele joined the militia and helped fend off the attacks. He continued his involvement in the militia even after the short war ended. In fact, he was so successful in organizing his fellow citizens in the town of Clarksburg, Ontario, that he was asked to become the commanding officer. Sam turned down the offer, believing he was too young for such a job. He was not yet twenty years old.

In 1869 Louis Riel headed up a Métis provisional government that was trying to protect native peoples from white settlers in what would soon become the province of Manitoba. After Riel had Thomas Scott executed in March 1870, the Canadian government took action to put down the rebellion. Two months later, Steele joined the combination of militia and regular army forces that would make the trek north and then west from Toronto. It was a long, difficult journey by train, steamship, canoe, and on foot. Steele amazed people with his physical strength, carrying loads of supplies that others could barely lift. The rebellion was all but over by the time Steele reached Manitoba, but his force stayed on to help patrol the area. During this time, Steele learned much about the people and the customs of the West. These lessons, too, would serve him well.

Steele remained in the regular army after returning to Ontario in 1871, but in 1873 he signed up with a brand-new police force created by the Canadian government. The North-West Mounted Police (forerunner of the Royal Canadian Mounted Police) would be responsible for patrolling the lands from Manitoba to British Columbia. Steele headed west to Fort Garry (future site of Winnipeg) and on November 3, 1873, he became the third man sworn in to the Mounties. The force had grown to 300 by July 8, when they left Manitoba for the great "March of 1874." Steele and the fifty men of A Troop travelled on foot and by horseback all the way to the Rocky Mountains, then north to Fort Edmonton. They covered more than 2,000 kilometres in two months, crossing rivers and struggling through forests on unmarked trails.

From 1875 to 1882, Sam Steele was assigned to several forts across the West, enduring hot Prairie summers and bone-chilling winters. He helped to negotiate treaties with the native peoples of the plains and earned a reputation for courage, toughness, and fairness that would become legendary.

In 1882 the men of the North-West Mounted Police were assigned to maintain law and justice along the route of the Canadian Pacific Railway. Steele and his men spent three years protecting railway workers as they toiled from Saskatchewan to British Columbia. The NWMP battled against the sale of illegal alcohol, crooked gamblers, and violent criminals. During the spring and summer of 1885, Steele was reassigned to help put down the second Riel Rebellion, but was back to see the completion of the CPR in the fall. He was present at Craigellachie, British Columbia, when Donald Smith drove in "the Last Spike." (See the biography of Donald Smith for more about this event.)

By 1885 Sam Steele held the rank of superintendent in the North-West Mounted Police. In 1887 he founded a new fort in the Kootenay region of British Columbia—it was named Fort Steele in his honour. In 1888 he moved on to Fort Macleod in southern Alberta, where he met Marie Harwood a year later. They were married in 1890.

In 1896 gold was discovered in the Klondike region of the Yukon Territory. On January 29, 1898, Sam Steele was ordered to go there. At this time, the border between Alaska and the Yukon was still in dispute. The government wanted Steele to protect Canadian interests and maintain law and order among the fortune seekers. Steele saw first-hand how difficult the job would be when he arrived in the town of Skagway, Alaska.

"Robbery and murder were daily occurrences," he later wrote in his memoirs. "Many people came there with money and next morning had not enough to get a meal, having been robbed or cheated out of their last cent. Shots were exchanged in broad daylight, and cries for help mingled with the cracked voices of the singers in the [music] halls at night."

Steele was determined that things would be different in Canadian territory. He would not outlaw alcohol and gambling, but he would make sure they were properly licensed. He also made sure that miners coming into the area had adequate provisions to get them through the long, difficult winters. When he saw more than 150 boats sink and ten people drown trying to ride the river to the goldfields in the spring of 1898, he established laws to regulate water travel. No other boats— or lives—were lost during his time there. That summer, Steele was promoted to lieutenant colonel and made commander of the Mounted Police in the Yukon. He moved into the NWMP post in Dawson City in September and began using fines collected from lawbreakers to help improve hospitals and sanitation. In the winter, a huge quantity of wood was needed for the fires that kept the town warm, and when the loss of money was not enough to convince men to go straight, Steele would sentence them to sixty days of chopping logs.

Sam Steele was recalled from the Yukon in September of 1899. When war broke out between England and the Boers in South Africa just one month later, he volunteered to serve in the Canadian Army. Donald Smith was raising a cavalry unit, Lord Strathcona's Horse, and he wanted Steele to lead his men into battle. The unit earned a reputation as one of the best and bravest battalions of the Boer War. At the end of the fighting, Steele was asked to stay on in South Africa to train a police force modelled on the North-West Mounted Police, and he commanded a division of the South African Constabulary until 1906. During much of that time, he also remained a member of the Canadian Mounties, retiring from the force in 1903 after thirty years of service.

Steele returned to Canada in 1906 and worked for the Canadian Army in the Prairie provinces. When the First World War broke out in 1914, he hoped to lead his troops into battle again, but he was considered too old to command a division. Instead, he was put in charge of Canadian troops at the British Army camp in Shorncliffe, England.

Steele retired from the army on July 1, 1918, shortly before the war ended. He was knighted by King George V for his service to the British Empire. Sadly, just a few months later, Sam Steele fell victim to the influenza epidemic that was sweeping the world. He died in England on January 30, 1919, but it was several months before his body could be shipped back to his home. Finally, in June of 1919, thousands of mourners in Winnipeg watched as Mounties in full uniform followed behind a riderless black horse. It was described as the largest funeral Western Canada had ever seen.

# Joseph-Elzéar Bernier
## 1852–1934

**D**URING MUCH OF HIS LENGTHY CAREER at sea, Joseph-Elzéar Bernier was called "the greatest Canadian navigator." He captained more than 100 ships during his lifetime, and crossed the Atlantic Ocean over 250 times. However, Bernier earned his greatest fame for his exploration of the Arctic. Most of this work was done for the Canadian government, studying the northern islands and establishing police posts there so that Canada could claim sovereignty of the area. The work was dangerous; many Arctic explorers had lost their lives in the harsh environment. However, when Sir Wilfrid Laurier expressed his concerns, Bernier told the

Canadian prime minister not to worry: "As my father and his father before him, I shall die in my bed."

Joseph-Elzéar Bernier was born into a seafaring family at L'Islet, Quebec, on New Year's Day in 1852. He was just two years old when he took to the sea for the first time, accompanying his parents to Cuba on a ship captained by his father. Shortly after that, young Joseph-Elzéar made his first journey across the Atlantic, accompanying his father, who was delivering a cargo of naval goods for the Crimean War in Russia. The boy remained at sea until he entered school at the age of seven. His formal education lasted only until he was twelve years old; then he went back to sea as a cabin boy on his father's ship. When he was seventeen, his father had a ship built for his son, and Joseph-Elzéar Bernier became, in his own words, "the youngest skipper in the world."

For the next twenty-six years, Bernier spent most of his time sailing ships around the world. He often delivered wooden ships built in Canada for sale in England. He also served time as the dockmaster of the Lauzon shipyard in Lévis, Quebec, and as the manager of the Dominion Ice Company, which provided ice for homes and businesses in Montreal. In 1895 Bernier became governor of the Quebec Jail. Though the job took him away from the sea for a while, he used his increased leisure time to investigate polar navigation. Using maps and charts, he devised a plan for reaching the North Pole—a feat that had not yet been accomplished.

Bernier's interest in the North Pole had been piqued back in 1871. He was in Connecticut that year when American explorer Charles Francis Hall left on his last polar expedition. From that point on, northern navigation became Bernier's primary interest. "My knowledge of ice conditions in the St. Lawrence and in the North Atlantic . . . led me to read up on the history of polar explorations in my spare time, and to study the problems of Arctic navigation. From 1872, my cabin library on shipboard consisted mainly of books on Arctic travel, and the latest Arctic maps were always in my chartroom."

After leaving the Quebec Jail in 1897, Bernier tried to convince the Canadian government of the importance of exploring the Arctic islands and perhaps discovering the North Pole. In 1904 he bought a ship for the government, which he called the *Arctic,* and prepared it for a five-year expedition. However, just as he was about to leave, the government sent him instead to Hudson Bay. Bernier sailed with a contingent from the Royal North-West Mounted Police, who were being sent there to settle a fishing dispute.

Bernier spent 1904–05 navigating Hudson Bay and helping to establish police posts along the shore. He finally got his chance to sail for the Arctic in 1906 but, again, issues of Canadian sovereignty would be more important than finding the North Pole. The British government had given Canada control of the Arctic islands in 1880; however, the young country had done nothing to formalize its control of the territory. Now, there was talk that American explorers might take possession of the islands for the United States. Bernier and his crew (which included several scientists) were dispatched to conduct topographic surveys of as many islands as they could visit, in order to help Canada establish its claim to the Arctic. The work was not as glamorous as searching for the North Pole (which was claimed by American Robert E. Peary in 1909), but Bernier took comfort from the idea that his work was important to Canada's future.

After 1906 Bernier made annual trips to the Arctic archipelago (a sea with many islands). He explored the territory, set up more police posts, and collected customs duties for the

Canadian government from the foreign whalers and traders working in the region. In 1908 he set sail from Quebec City with orders to travel as far north as possible. The Prince of Wales (soon to be King George V of England) was on hand to see Bernier off on his mission. The following year, Bernier claimed Baffin Island for Canada, with a unique ceremony of his own invention. "I took possession of Baffin Island for Canada in the presence of several [Inuit]," Bernier wrote. "After firing nineteen shots (into the air), I instructed an [Inuit] to fire the twentieth, telling him he was now a Canadian." A similar ceremony was conducted on Melville Island on July 1, 1909, when Bernier claimed the whole of the Arctic archipelago for Canada. An official plaque was also unveiled.

Bernier's ceremonies reflected his times, when the native inhabitants of the land being "claimed" were not consulted. In fact, negotiations with the Inuit over land rights and other issues would go on for decades. However, Bernier's actions had ensured that it would be Canada, and not any other country, that would be responsible for these negotiations.

Bernier continued to make voyages on behalf of the Canadian government until 1911. After that, he went into private business, trading on Baffin Island and searching for gold. However, the outbreak of the First World War in 1914 ended all Arctic expeditions for some time. Bernier was now in his mid-sixties, but he spent the war years delivering mail along the shores of the St. Lawrence River and the coast of Labrador. He also made several transport voyages across the ocean to Europe. After the war and until he retired in 1925, he patrolled the eastern Arctic for the Canadian government.

Joseph-Elzéar Bernier was now seventy-three years old, but his retirement did not last for long. In 1927 the Canadian government asked him to return to Hudson Bay. This time, he was sent to study whether grain grown on the Canadian Prairies could be shipped through the port of Churchill, on the shores of Hudson Bay. The route he plotted would eventually allow ships to carry twenty million bushels of wheat per year. Bernier made his final trip to Hudson Bay in 1929, and then he retired for good at the age of seventy-seven. He spent the next five years living quietly in Lévis, until he passed away the day after Christmas in 1934. As he had once reassured Prime Minister Laurier, Bernier died peacefully in his own bed. Five years later, an autobiography he had written was published.

# Robert Borden
## 1854–1937

R OBERT BORDEN WAS BORN in the peaceful village of Grand Pré, Nova Scotia. The boy who would grow up to become a prime minister of Canada was raised on a farm, and did his share of the haying, hoeing, and other chores. The farm was close enough to the sea that young Robert could hear the surf on the shore as he fell asleep at night. The Borden family loved books, and Robert began to read early. He became an excellent student, and one day, when his teacher suddenly quit after an argument with the principal, the principal asked Robert to teach the class. He was only fourteen and some of his students were older than he was. That was the end of his formal schooling, although he continued to educate himself. For the next five years, he held teaching jobs at private schools in Nova Scotia and New Jersey.

Borden then decided to become a lawyer, and in 1874 he got a job as a clerk in an important Halifax law firm. For the next four years, Borden worked in the law office from nine in the morning until six in the evening, then studied law at home at night. In 1877 he took the exams that would allow him to become a lawyer and received the top marks in his class. His marks were even better than those of Charles Hibbert Tupper, who had studied law at Harvard University. In 1882 he joined a law practice with Tupper, whose father (also named Charles) would later be a prime minister.

By the 1890s, Borden had become a leading lawyer in Nova Scotia. In April of 1896, he was in Ottawa to argue a case before the Supreme Court when Sir Charles Tupper, just before his brief term as prime minister, invited Borden to dinner. Tupper convinced him that he should run for Parliament in the upcoming election. Tupper's Conservative Party wound up losing the election, but Borden won his Halifax riding.

Borden quickly earned a reputation as a hard-working Member of Parliament, and soon Tupper was using him to speak on various issues in the House of Commons. But Liberal Sir Wilfrid Laurier had become a very popular prime minister, and the Conservative Party suffered. When they were beaten badly in the next election in 1900, Sir Charles Tupper resigned as leader. Charles Hibbert Tupper, with his father's permission, asked Borden to consider the job. Borden was not sure that he was the right choice, but in February of 1901 he agreed to become leader of the Conservative Party.

Borden was intelligent and hard working, but compared to the charismatic Laurier, he seemed dull and uninteresting.

When the Conservatives were again defeated in the election of 1904, Borden offered to resign as leader, but the party voted for him to stay on. After another election loss in 1908, circumstances finally began changing in Borden's favour.

By 1909 Britain, worried that Germany's strong navy was a threat to its safety, asked Canada and the other British colonies to help support the Royal Navy. Prime Minister Laurier decided that Canada should start its own navy. Borden thought that a Canadian navy could help the country earn a more important voice in the British Empire, but much of Canada saw a separate navy as a sign of disloyalty to England. Since most members of the Conservative Party wanted Canada to send money to help the Royal Navy, Borden decided to support this view.

When Laurier went ahead with a Canadian Navy in 1910, much of the support for the Liberals began to shift to the Conservatives—and it shifted even further when Laurier's government proposed a free-trade deal with the United States. The deal would eliminate the tariffs (taxes) that made American goods more costly to buy in Canada, but much of the country saw "Reciprocity" as a further weakening of Canada's ties to England. There were also fears that the United States might gain too much control of the country. Reciprocity became the main issue in the general election of 1911. This time the Conservatives won, and Robert Borden became prime minister.

Though he had opposed Reciprocity in the election, Borden recognized the importance of Canada's relationship with the United States. Two months after he was elected, Borden visited New York to assure important businessmen that he was not anti-American and that Canada still welcomed trade with the United States.

Early in 1912 Borden went to London to meet with Winston Churchill, the politician in charge of the Royal Navy. Churchill expressed great concern over the growing strength of the German navy. Borden felt that the new Canadian Navy—which still had only two ships—would be of little help to England if there was a war. His plan was to have Canada contribute $35 million towards the building of new British battleships. Even though the Liberals eventually blocked its passing, Borden's Naval Aid Bill angered the voters in Quebec who had supported him in the last election.

In June 1914 Canada's prime minister accepted a knighthood from King George V, and became Sir Robert Borden. Two months later, the German army marched through Belgium on its way to attack France. On August 4, 1914, England declared war on Germany, and because it was part of the British Empire, Canada was at war as well.

At first, Canadians across the country supported the war. By October, Canada had trained 30,000 volunteers to join the British war effort. But as more and more Canadian soldiers made their way overseas, Borden became frustrated by way the British government failed to consult the Canadian government about its military plans. He argued that Canada could not be expected to "put 400,000 or 500,000 men in the field and willingly accept the position of having no more voice and receiving no more consideration than if we were toy automata [robots]."

As the First World War dragged on, the British government came to realize how much it needed Canada. In March of 1917, Borden arrived in London to meet with England's prime minister and other colonial leaders as part of an Imperial War Cabinet. Borden was pleased that Canada would now have a voice in the decision-making process, but he wanted more. He wanted a promise that Canada and the other countries would continue to have a say in world affairs after the war. This promise became known as Resolution IX and it marked a significant step towards full Canadian nationhood.

When Borden returned to Canada in May, he felt that support for the British war effort was more important than ever. He also believed that the Canadian soldiers who had fought so valiantly in battles like the one at Vimy Ridge deserved the country's support. (For more about this battle, see the biography of Arthur Currie.) But Canadian citizens were no longer volunteering in large enough numbers, so Borden was going to have to introduce Conscription—a plan to draft men between the ages of twenty and forty-five into the army. Borden knew that Conscription would be unpopular in Quebec, where Canada's role in the war was now seen as putting England's interests ahead of its own. In order to help sell Conscription to Quebec, Borden hoped to convince Laurier to join him in a coalition government. The coalition would give equal representation to Conservatives and Liberals, but Laurier believed it was wrong to force anyone to fight. Still, many Liberals supported Conscription, and they joined the Conservatives in a Union government.

Conscription was introduced in August of 1917. By November, more than 321,000 men had registered, but over 310,000 of them claimed there were reasons why they should not have to join the army. An election was called for December, and Conscription was the only issue. In order to ensure a win for the Union government, Borden let the soldiers overseas mail votes back to Canada. Women had never been allowed to vote in federal elections before, but Borden now gave the vote to women with husbands or children in the army. On the other hand, immigrants who had come to Canada within the last fifteen years from countries that were now the enemy were stripped of their right to vote. Not surprisingly, the Union government won in a landslide. Support for the Liberals came only from Quebec.

By the time the First World War ended in November 1918, almost 620,000 Canadians had fought in the war. About 60,000 had been killed and more than 173,000 were injured. When it came time to negotiate a peace treaty, Borden insisted that Canada must be allowed to take part. Although England, France, the United States, and Italy made most of the decisions at the Paris Peace Conference, Canada was able to earn recognition as an emerging, independent country. When it came time to sign the Treaty of Versailles, Borden refused to accept the idea that the King's signature should be good enough for the entire British Empire. He called a special session of Parliament in September of 1919 in order for Canada to approve the treaty itself.

Sir Robert Borden was left exhausted by the political battles he had fought both during and after the First World War. In July of 1920, he resigned as leader of the Conservative Party, though he did stay on as the Member of Parliament for his Nova Scotia riding until the next election, in 1921. In retirement, he became an elder statesman, always willing to listen and offer advice to politicians of any party. He began to give lectures and publish essays. He served as the Canadian representative on several British delegations and as a Canadian member of the League of Nations (forerunner of the United Nations). Borden, who had always valued education, was proud to be Chancellor of Queen's University in Kingston, Ontario, from 1924 until 1930. In 1936, only a year before his death, eighty-two-year-old Robert Borden travelled to France to visit Canada's war graves and to be present at the unveiling of the Vimy War Memorial.

# Ned Hanlan
## 1855–1908

S HOWERS GREETED THE MORNING of November 15, 1880, but the rain and fog failed to dampen the enthusiasm of the crowd. Rowing was the most popular sport in the world, and more than 100,000 people lined the shore of the 4-mile, 440-yard (about 7-km) course. Some were in boats; others crowded onto the three bridges that crossed the Thames River in the city of London, England. The race for the World Championship would be contested by two British colonials—an Australian and a Canadian. Australian sports fans had combined to wager $100,000 on their oarsman. The city of Toronto alone had raised $42,000 to back their man. On one single day before the race, $20,000 in bets came in from New York. These were staggering sums of money at the time.

Ned Hanlan was the darling of rowing fans in Canada, the United States, and England. But at just five foot, nine inches and 155 pounds, how could he possibly be strong enough to beat the Australian giant? Edward Trickett stood six foot, four inches and weighed over 200 pounds. Yet, at the starting line, it was Trickett—the self-proclaimed World Champion—who looked nervous. Hanlan, in his trademark blue jersey, was calm as he awaited the starter's signal. The race began shortly after noon. Trickett, with his powerful arms, slapped at the water with forty strokes per minute. Hanlan, with his more graceful style, averaged only thirty-six, but by the end of the first mile, he already had a comfortable lead.

In the days leading up to the World Championship race, Hanlan had been angered by the Australian's boastful taunting. Hanlan was never shy about having a little fun, and now he was going to teach Trickett a lesson.

One third of the way into the race, Hanlan stopped rowing. Trickett pulled furiously on his oars, but just as he caught up, Hanlan pulled in front again. Once he'd regained a three-length lead, Hanlan rowed over near the shore to acknowledge his fans. Later in the race, he stopped again to chat with an old rival he had not seen in a year. Then he stopped and pretended to take a drink of water from the river. But every time Trickett pulled closer, Hanlan would speed away again. Then, near the end of the race, Hanlan appeared to collapse. He slumped forward in his boat, oars drifting in the water, slowing him down. Seeing his chance, Trickett summoned a final burst of energy. But when he had almost pulled even, Hanlan sat up, flashed a smile at the Australian, and sped off. Towards the end of the race, he rowed with only one hand—first his right, then his left—zig-zagging to the finish line. Ned Hanlan of Canada was Champion of the World.

Edward "Ned" Hanlan was born on Toronto Island, in the city's harbour on Lake Ontario. His father had been a fisherman, but now operated a hotel on the island. Young Ned would often accompany his father when he went fishing or while he ferried guests to and from the hotel. By the age of five, Ned could already row across Toronto Bay. Soon, he was paddling to the mainland to attend school. When he got older, Ned helped his father in the hotel and spent his spare time practising his rowing technique in a makeshift shell. At the age of sixteen, in 1871, he entered his first race. In 1873 he beat several prominent local scullers to win the championship of Toronto Bay. In 1875 he won the Ontario Championship.

Until this point, Hanlan had been rowing in amateur competitions. Occasionally he had earned money by betting on himself to win, but soon there would be much bigger paydays. Hanlan had attracted the attention of several prominent Toronto businessmen who saw the financial value of his success. These men formed the Hanlan Club, an organization that would look after the details of arranging races, so that Ned could concentrate on developing his skills. The club was responsible for a major rowing innovation that would become the key to Hanlan's success—a sliding seat in his shell. The sliding seat allowed a rower's body to move back and forth as he stroked. The longer strokes that this technique allowed increased the boat's speed. Hanlan was the first to master this skill, which he demonstrated in 1876 at a regatta in Philadelphia.

This race in Philadelphia was part of the celebrations marking the centennial of the United States. It offered a prize of $800, but, even more important, it offered Hanlan a chance to test his skill in an international competition. He won the race handily, toying with the top Americans in much the same way he would later beat Edward Trickett. He returned to Toronto as a hero, greeted with parades and civic receptions. Hanlan was just twenty-one years old, but his fame was spreading.

Rowing fever had first hit Canada in the earliest days of Confederation, when an upstart crew of four men from New Brunswick defeated the best rowers from England, France, and America at an 1867 regatta in Paris. Ten years later, the country was abuzz over a Canadian Championship battle between Ned Hanlan and New Brunswick's Wallace Ross. The race was scheduled for Toronto Bay on October 13, 1877. Railways announced special rates to bring visitors into the city, and steamboat companies offered choice seats on their ships along the course. Bad weather delayed the race for two days, but 25,000 people were on hand when the race was finally staged on October 15. Hanlan was in control throughout. With a ten-length lead late in the race, he began blowing kisses to the crowd. Ross fell further and further behind, and "The Boy in Blue" surged to a thirty-length victory.

The Canadian Championship carried a prize of $1,000, but Hanlan earned even more money from the bets he won. When he took the American Championship in 1878, it was said that the group of fifty-four Torontonians who followed him to Pittsburgh had bet a total of $60,000 on the race. With the huge amounts of money gamblers were wagering on races, there was often speculation that the results might be fixed. It did appear that some of the men Hanlan beat would sometimes bet on themselves to lose, but no one ever accused Ned of doing anything wrong. Actually, because of his great skill, people joked that the only reason Hanlan might need to pay someone off was to make sure that they showed up for the race.

Despite his success in North America, Hanlan was not yet known in England, where few expected that a rower from the colonies could beat the best of Britain. He proved the doubters wrong on June 16, 1879. Not only did he win the race by eleven boat lengths, he knocked 55 seconds off the previous record time over the 5-mile (8-km) course. Hanlan was now the most famous Canadian in the world; however, because he held the national title in three different countries, people often wondered exactly where he was from. American newspapers liked to claim him for their own, but as Hanlan told reporters in New York, on his way back to Toronto from London: "I am a Canadian."

Hanlan's fame continued to spread after he won the World Championship in 1880. He held the title until August 16, 1884, when he was finally beaten by a man named William Beach in a race in Australia. Despite his loss, Hanlan continued to compete until the age of forty-two. In all, records have been found for more than 300 Hanlan races, and they show that he was beaten only six times.

After his retirement, Ned Hanlan represented the Toronto Islands as an alderman at city hall in 1898 and 1899. When he died of pneumonia on January 4, 1908, the city of Toronto held a special civic funeral, and more than 10,000 people paid their last respects to him. In 1926 a statue was unveiled in his honour on the grounds of the Canadian National Exhibition.

# Kit Coleman
## 1856–1915

KATHLEEN FERGUSON, who would one day become Kit Coleman, a pioneering newspaper reporter, was born in Castleblakeney, Ireland. She was raised in a middle-class family that owned seventy-five acres of farmland as well as a popular pub. Kathleen, an avid reader, was well educated at an Irish girls school and then at a boarding school in Belgium. But then her happy, privileged life began to come apart. At the age of sixteen, she was pushed into marriage by her parents. Her new husband was a man she did not love, a merchant named Thomas Willis who was forty years her senior. Their daughter died at the age of two and, shortly after, Willis was killed in a riding accident. The widow then left Ireland, determined to make a new life for herself.

After a brief stint as a governess in London, she emigrated to Toronto, Ontario, in 1884. There, she chose her own husband, but she did no better than her parents had: Edward Watkins was a layabout and a heavy drinker. They had two children, and then Kathleen divorced him. She returned to working as a governess to support herself and her children. For extra income, she wrote two short articles, signed them "Kit," and sent them off to a Toronto newspaper, the *Daily Mail.* To her delight, the newspaper published both. A new weekly magazine, *Saturday Night,* also accepted three stories by Kit.

Christopher Bunting, the managing editor of the *Daily Mail,* had been looking for someone to write a weekly women's page. He had in mind notes about fashion and cooking and other "feminine" topics. But Kit turned her column, called "Woman's Kingdom," into something much broader. Today, a newspaper's feature writer might produce a weekly column of about 800 words. "Woman's Kingdom" was often ten times that length. Kit wrote about everything that interested her: politics, or wonderful new inventions such as the telephone and the "Cinematographe" (movies), or the wretched working conditions of garment workers, who were mostly women. From time to time, she actually did write about the latest fashions, although usually in a humorous way.

At the end of Kit's column was a section that quickly became the most popular: her answers to letters from her readers. Sometimes gentle and sometimes tough, Kit gave out advice to the "lovelorn"—or, as we might say today, people having trouble with their relationships. To a confused young woman, Kit wrote sternly, "He engages you to marry him, then directly finds out you have lost some of your money, so he jilts you. Then Fortune smiles on you and he comes whining back. How could you think of marrying such a flabby poltroon?"

From the beginning, "Woman's Kingdom" was a hit. At first, people were unsure whether Kit was a man or a woman, but eventually, the secret came out and Kit became a local celebrity. Many readers turned first to her column, to see what she would say next. Kit used her new power at the newspaper to win more interesting assignments. In 1893 she covered the Columbian Exposition (forerunner of modern World's Fairs) in Chicago. She wrote of the wondrous electric lights that flooded the fair with light after sundown. On assignment in Ottawa two years later, she introduced herself to Prime Minister Wilfrid Laurier. He was charmed by her wit and intelligence. When the *Mail and Empire* (her paper's new name) sent her to London in 1897 for Queen Victoria's Diamond Jubilee, Laurier made sure she had a good seat in the viewing stand for the royal procession. He even brought her along on an official visit to the Queen. Kit wasn't overly impressed. "The Royal Family has dreadful taste in furnishing their palaces," she wrote. "Can you imagine anything more hideous than walls and windows hung with tartan?"

Kit, now in her forties and with ten years of journalism behind her, was determined to report on something more important than the Queen's curtains. In 1898 she persuaded her paper to send her to Cuba, where a war between the United States and Spain was underway. She was the first woman in history to be an accredited (official) war correspondent. Kit got as far as Florida and then military red tape kept her away from Cuba until the fighting was almost over. However, she sent back vivid eyewitness reports of wounded soldiers, wrecked ships, and dazed civilians. Many newspapers reprinted her reports, and Kit became world famous.

For several years, Kit had been courted by a doctor from Seaforth, Ontario, named Theobald Coleman. After her unhappy experiences, she was hesitant to marry again, but the kind and patient Coleman won her over. When she returned from Cuba, they were married. She continued to write "Woman's Kingdom," now signed "Kit Coleman." She also continued to travel and cover the big stories, including the San Francisco Earthquake in 1906.

For all her success, Kit Coleman faced discrimination as a woman. She was never invited to the *Mail and Empire*'s annual dinners, which were men-only events. Despite her friendship with Sir Wilfrid Laurier, she could not report on the proceedings of Parliament. That was the job of the Parliamentary Press Gallery, and women were not allowed to be members. To give women journalists a place to network and discuss issues of importance to them, Kit Coleman helped to found the Canadian Women's Press Club. She was its first president in 1904.

In 1911 Kit asked the *Mail and Empire* for a $5-a-week raise. The new managing editor said no, and she resigned. However, she continued to write a syndicated column (a column sold to a number of newspapers). Again, Kit was a pioneer. She was the first syndicated columnist in Canada, and she was soon making more money than she had at the *Mail and Empire*. In 1915 the hard-working journalist caught a cold that developed into pneumonia. To the shock and sadness of her faithful readers, Kit Coleman died on May 26 at the age of fifty-nine.

# Adelaide Hunter Hoodless

## 1857–1910

BECAUSE OF A PERSONAL TRAGEDY, Adelaide Hunter Hoodless's life was completely transformed—and so were the lives of countless other Canadian women.

Adelaide Sophia Hunter was born and raised on a farm near St. George, Canada West (later Ontario). She was the youngest of twelve children, and her father died a few months before she was born. Everyone in the family had to work hard to keep the family farm running. Her life became easier at the age of twenty-four, when she married John Hoodless, a successful furniture manufacturer, and they moved to Hamilton, Ontario.

Adelaide Hoodless eventually gave birth to four children, and the family enjoyed a happy middle-class life. Then, in 1889, her youngest child, eighteen-month-old John Harold, suddenly died. In those times, it was not unusual for children to die—in the late 1800s, one in five Canadian children died before reaching adulthood. What was unusual was Adelaide Hoodless's response to this tragedy. She closely questioned the doctor who had attended her son. She learned that the boy probably died from drinking contaminated milk, which could have happened if the milk had been left where flies could land on it and spread disease.

Hoodless was determined to prevent further such needless deaths if she could. It seemed to her that the key was better-informed mothers. In her time, women were almost totally responsible for the health of their families. Doctors were rarely called; women depended on shared knowledge of prevention and remedies. There were no packaged pre-cooked foods; families ate well only if women prepared nutritious meals. Many women were also responsible for the family budget. Hoodless devoted the rest of her life to better education for women about motherhood and "domestic science" (household management).

The first campaign she led was a drive to have milk in the Hamilton area pasteurized—a treatment that would kill bacteria. In 1889 she became the first president of the Young Women's Christian Association (YWCA) when it opened in Hamilton; a few years later she became president of the national YWCA. At the Hamilton Y, she began teaching a domestic-science course in which she covered nutrition, sanitation, and household finances. Young women flocked to the program.

From 1894 to 1896 Hoodless travelled across the province at the request of Ontario's education minister. In each community, she informed people about the importance of domestic-science courses. She urged them to establish these courses in their local public schools. Within a few years, as a result of her efforts, domestic science was added to the school curriculum not only in Ontario, but also in New Brunswick, Nova Scotia, Manitoba, and British Columbia. She wrote a textbook for the new courses.

Hoodless found that she had a talent for forceful and persuasive public speaking. At the annual "Ladies' Night" of the Farmers' Institute in 1897, she addressed the men bluntly: "You are in the midst of a campaign to improve the health of your animals. I am here to tell you the health of your wives and children is more important." Then she suggested that rural women should have an institute of their own. She had never forgotten the hard, often isolated lives of farm women that she had seen first-hand while growing up.

One week later, over a hundred women showed up at Hoodless's founding meeting of the first Women's Institute in the world, in Stoney Creek, Ontario. Women's Institutes became a powerful influence for good in the lives of rural Canadian women—and their children. The Institutes provided libraries, medical and dental clinics, meeting rooms, and space for drama and singing groups. They had guest speakers on such subjects as cooking, dressmaking, and home nursing. They also provided services for immigrant women, to help them adjust to their new country. Within a few years, Women's Institutes had spread across Canada and around the world. Today Canada's Women's Institutes are part of the Associated Country Women of the World, which has 8.5 million members worldwide.

Later, Hoodless worked with Lady Aberdeen, the wife of the governor general of Canada and a woman with a strong social conscience. In 1897 Lady Aberdeen founded the Victorian Order of Nurses (VON), to supply visiting nurses for people without access to doctors and hospitals. Hoodless established the second chapter of the VON in Hamilton in 1899. Today the Victorian

Order of Nurses is a national non-profit organization that provides home-care nursing. Again with Lady Aberdeen, Hoodless helped to found the National Council of Women, and was its first treasurer.

In 1903 Hoodless persuaded tobacco magnate Sir William Macdonald to establish the Macdonald Institute at the Ontario Agricultural College (later the University of Guelph). Here—and at another Macdonald College which opened later near Montreal—Canadian women could train to teach domestic science.

Hoodless faced criticism because she was a wife and mother from a well-off family who made public speeches and was often away from home. "Let her stay home and take care of her own family," her critics said. However, her own family completely supported her causes. Hoodless herself held traditional views about women: despite her own public life, she truly believed that a woman's place was in the home, not in the larger world. She had no interest, for example, in the campaign to give women the vote.

Hoodless worked tirelessly until her death, which occurred very suddenly when she had a heart attack while delivering a speech. She was only fifty-two years old. A Canadian stamp was issued in her honour in 1993, and her childhood home near St. George, Ontario, is now a museum maintained by the Federated Women's Institutes of Canada.

# Joseph Burr Tyrrell
## 1858–1957

I N THE SPRING OF 1884, twenty-five-year-old Joseph Burr
Tyrrell came to the Badlands of what is now Alberta to
look for coal deposits. He and his assistant paddled a
canoe down the Red Deer River, checking the exposed rock
faces that rose on either side. Tyrrell spotted seams of coal in
the exposed rock faces—and then he saw something else. An
odd brown object was sticking out of the valley wall. He clam-
bered up the steep slope and cleared away the dirt around the
object with his bare hands and geologist's hammer. He realized
that he had found the bones of some ancient creature. As
Tyrrell explored the area in the next few days, he came upon

more and more bones. But the most dramatic encounter was still to come.

Tyrrell still remembered it vividly when he was in his nineties: "I was climbing up a steep face about 400 feet [120 metres] high. I stuck my head around a point, and there was this skull leering at me, sticking right out of the ground. It gave me a fright." Dinosaurs had been recognized by science as a group of extinct animals only forty years earlier. Few people knew much about them. But Tyrrell realized at once that he had found something that should be seen by experts.

Tyrrell had some of the fossil bones he found, including the skull, loaded onto a buckboard and taken to Fort Calgary. From there, the bones were shipped to Ottawa so that scientists could study them. They determined that the huge skull found by Tyrrell was about 70 million years old. It belonged to a dinosaur now called Albertosaurus, a meat-eating relative of Tyrannosaurus Rex; it was the first of these creatures ever found.

Soon, paleontologists (scientists who study the remains of ancient creatures) from around the world flocked to the area to claim dinosaur specimens for natural history museums. Since then, the bones of close to 500 dinosaurs have been unearthed there. Today, the Royal Tyrrell Museum of Paleontology, named for Joseph Burr Tyrrell, stands near the site of his first discovery. The man who made what is often called "the world's richest paleontological discovery" was not himself a paleontologist. He was, however, a geologist, a mineralogist, a cartographer (map-maker), and one of Canada's most intrepid land explorers.

Joseph Burr Tyrrell was born in Weston, Canada West (later Ontario), the son of prosperous Irish immigrants. He was an undersized and sickly boy, and a childhood bout of scarlet fever impaired both his eyesight and his hearing. However, he loved the outdoor life, and fortunately the family doctor encouraged him, believing that fresh air would "strengthen his lungs." Tyrrell hiked along the Humber River, collecting insects, turtles, and crayfish, including one that he kept for a while in the family bathtub. In the barn, he kept white mice and rabbits. His eyesight corrected with glasses and his aim steady, he also learned to be a crack shot. Although he never killed animals for sport, his marksmanship would one day save his life.

After earning a degree from the University of Toronto, Tyrrell joined the Geological Survey of Canada in 1881. This is one of Canada's oldest scientific departments, founded in 1841, when "Canada" referred only to what is now Ontario and Quebec. The department's mission was to gather knowledge about Canada's land mass and mineral resources. In the spring of 1884, the Geological Survey sent Tyrrell to explore the Badlands of Alberta. He found not only dinosaur bones, but also Canada's largest coal deposit.

In the summer of 1893 Tyrrell made one of the most ambitious land journeys in Canadian history. After studying the journeys that Samuel Hearne had made in the eighteenth century, Tyrrell was determined to cross the Barren Grounds of the North. Beginning at Lake Athabaska, Tyrrell and seven companions, including his brother, headed to Hudson Bay, then south to Winnipeg, and back home. Travelling by canoe, dogsled, and, for nearly 1,500 kilometres, snowshoes, Tyrrell's party covered 5,150 kilometres. Almost half of this had never been surveyed. On the first leg of the journey, the party almost died of cold and starvation, nearly 500 kilometres from Churchill, the closest settlement, on Hudson Bay. Tyrrell finally managed to shoot a polar bear (his marksmanship had paid off), and the explorers were so hungry that they ate it right down to its innards and the contents of its stomach. It took the party another month to reach Churchill. After taking a few

days to recover, Tyrrell set out on the next leg of the journey—
1,500 kilometres—to reach Winnipeg.

In February 1894, Tyrrell married Edith Carey, known to her
family as "Dollie," whom he had been courting, off and on,
between expeditions, for several years. Soon, though, Tyrrell was
back in the Barren Lands to survey and map the vast area.
Throughout their marriage, the restless Tyrrell would often be
gone for months at a time.

In 1897 Tyrrell presented a paper on glaciation to a scientific
conference. His theory—that glaciers had spread and retreated
several times in Canada's ancient past—was controversial at the
time, but is now accepted. But Tyrrell was growing disillusioned
with the Geological Survey of Canada: he felt that the department
had gone out of its way to deny him credit for his discoveries.
Furthermore, after many years of service, he was still classified as
a clerk and was earning less than $1,800 a year. In 1898, during the
Kondike gold rush in the Yukon, he saw a miner scoop his pan
into the gravel of a riverbed and bring out gold worth more than
a third of Tyrrell's annual salary.

Tyrrell left the Geological Survey in 1899 and went to work
as a consultant in the Klondike. As a geologist, he could advise
others on likely places to stake claims. When the Yukon gold
rush ended, he helped to locate and exploit cobalt and silver
deposits in Northern Ontario. By 1924 he had become president
of the Kirkland Lake Gold Mining Company—and a very
wealthy man.

In 1934 Tyrrell was told by his doctor that his exploring days
were over. He had arthritis and a heart condition. However, soon
afterward, at the age of seventy-eight, he joined one last gold
rush, this time to Yellowknife in the Northwest Territories.

Tyrrell was a member of the Champlain Society, which
publishes important documents about Canadian history. For

the society, he edited the journals of David Thompson and Samuel Hearne and made Canadians aware of the feats of those two early explorers, whose lives and achievements had been almost forgotten. He was awarded the Geological Society of London's Wollaston Medal, a rare honour that had also been awarded to Charles Darwin. At the age of ninety-four, Tyrrell was still the very active president of the Kirkland Lake Gold Mining Company. He died at the age of ninety-eight at his home in Toronto.

# E. Cora Hind
## 1861–1942

THE WOMAN DRESSED IN RIDING BREECHES, a fringed buckskin jacket, and a Stetson hat was a familiar figure in Prairie farming communities. She road the train from place to place. At each stop, she got out and looked around the wheatfields, scaling fences if she needed to. She gathered up heads of wheat and threshed them in her hands to see how fat the kernels were, and she checked the stalks for any sign of disease.

E. Cora Hind had been doing this for several years, but in 1904 her survey had particular importance. Chicago wheat experts were reporting that a plague of black rust—a grain disease—would ruin the Canadian crop. They predicted that the Prairies would produce only 35 million bushels of wheat. Back in the days before the Canadian Wheat Board set prices, investors used to speculate in grain. Knowing how big a crop was expected was vital in figuring out what price to pay. Millions of dollars were at stake. Hind thought the Chicago estimate was ridiculously low—her inspection showed her that although some fields were diseased, many were healthy. She released her own prediction in the *Winnipeg Free Press*: 55 million bushels. When the grain was harvested, the yield came in at 54 million. Hind was hailed as the greatest wheat expert in the West.

Ella Cora Hind began her life far from the Prairies. She was born in Toronto, where her father was a stonemason, carving figures for cathedrals and public buildings. However, both her parents died when she was a small child. With her two brothers, she moved to a farm in Grey County and was raised by her father's unmarried sister, Alice Hind, and her grandfather. Despite the loss of her parents, she had a happy childhood with these loving relatives. As she made the rounds of the farm with her grandfather, she first learned about crops and livestock. However, she had no idea how useful this knowledge was going to be.

Hind finished grade school and high school and then wrote an examination to become a teacher. She had no great interest in the schoolroom, but she needed and wanted to work, and few careers were welcoming to a woman in the 1880s. What she really wanted to do was write for a newspaper, but she saw little chance of doing that. Then two male cousins stopped by the farm— they were just back from Winnipeg and excited by the opportunities there. Alice and Cora Hind would have no trouble finding jobs in this young and growing city, they said. Ready for a change in their lives, both women headed west. Tucked in her suitcase, Hind had a letter of introduction to W.F. Luxton, editor of the *Manitoba Free Press* (later the *Winnipeg Free Press*), written by her uncle George, who was a friend of Luxton's.

Winnipeg was a raw, new community when the two women arrived in August 1882. The earthen streets turned to sticky, boot-grabbing mud when it rained. Many buildings were just tarpaper shacks, and some people lived in tents. But Main Street already had some elegant three- and four-storey buildings. Mail service had just begun, and two months after the Hinds arrived, the first traffic light was installed. Alice Hind quickly found work as a dressmaker, but Cora Hind's hopes were just as quickly dashed.

W.F. Luxton welcomed Hind to his office, but made it clear that he would not consider hiring a woman. Hind was discouraged but not defeated. She would write articles for the paper, even if Luxton would not hire her full-time. The first article she submitted was published, but anonymously. Luxton could not bring himself to print an article signed by a woman.

Meanwhile, Hind had discovered another line of work. Typewriters—then called typewriting machines—were just coming into use in offices. Women, she heard, were being hired to operate them. But there were still no typewriting machines and no type-writers (the people who worked on them) in Winnipeg. Then Hind discovered a dealer in Winnipeg with thirty of the machines that he hadn't yet sold. On one of his machines, she taught herself to type. When he finally sold a typewriting machine, he told her who had bought it—it was the law firm of Sir John A. Macdonald's son, Hugh John, and his partner. So, she presented herself at their offices, as a type-writer who could handle their paperwork. She got the job, at $6 per week (a little over $100 a week in today's dollars). Hind stayed at the law firm until 1893, gradually taking on more responsibility for running the office. She was always proud to point out that she was the first Canadian typist west of the Great Lakes.

In 1893 Cora Hind went into business for herself. She set up a stenographer's bureau where people could come to dictate their business letters and have them professionally typed. Farmers, merchants, and visiting business people came to Hind's office. Chatting with them, she began to learn a great deal about the economy of Western Canada. Hind had a wonderful memory and absorbed every useful fact she heard. In the 1890s, it was Canadian government policy to attract European immigrants to the Prairies with offers of free farmland. Settlers were pouring in from Poland, Scandinavia, Ukraine, and other European countries. The wheat yield was growing dramatically each year, and Winnipeg had become the prosperous centre of the Western wheat trade.

The Manitoba Dairy Association, which had used Hind's typing services, asked her to be its recording secretary at a convention. She not only recorded their meetings, she sent a report about the association to the *Winnipeg Free Press*. Over the next few years, Hind wrote more and more agricultural reports for the *Press*. Soon she was writing articles for American papers, too. One newspaper wanted her to sign her name "E.C. Hind," but she refused. It was to be "E. Cora Hind," so that everyone would know the writer was a woman. Hind was always a strong supporter of political equality for women—she worked with Nellie McClung and others in the long campaign to gain Manitoba women the right to vote. (See Nellie McClung's biography for more about this campaign.)

In 1895 a Toronto magazine publisher hired Hind to make a survey of the Western wheat crop. The weather had been wet and dismal all summer, and the publisher wanted to know whether it was true that the crop would be a failure. Hind set off by train across the Canadian West. In each community she would check farmers' fields on all sides of the train station. Then she would re-board and repeat the exercise at the next stop. When she had finished her survey, she was able to report that there was plenty of healthy grain for a successful harvest. She turned out to be correct, and her reputation was launched.

In 1901 the *Winnipeg Free Press* had a new editor, John Wesley Dafoe, who was happy to hire Cora Hind as a reporter specializing in agriculture. It had been twenty years since she first applied for a job at the paper.

Now E. Cora Hind was becoming a legend in the West for the amazing accuracy of her harvest predictions. In 1907 she predicted 71,259,000 bushels, and was only off by 337,000; in 1909 she predicted 188,109,000 bushels and was only off by 10,000. She also wrote knowledgeable articles about beef cattle, sheep breeding, and many other agricultural subjects, and her fame spread around the world. In 1922, on a trip to England, she successfully campaigned to get the British government to lift a ban against Canadian cattle, which were falsely believed to be carrying disease. Even into her seventies, she was still clambering over fences in July and August, checking the wheat crop.

Among the adventures she undertook in her seventies was a voyage on the first cargo ship to carry Prairie wheat out of the port of Churchill. Three years later, she left on a two-year trip around the world, visiting twenty-seven wheat-producing countries and reporting back to readers of the *Free Press*. When she died at age eighty-one, she was still on staff at the newspaper— and working on an article.

# E. Pauline Johnson
## 1861–1913

**P**AULINE JOHNSON was one of the most celebrated poets and performers of her day. Her achievement was doubly unusual: she supported herself by giving public performances at a time when most women stayed quietly in their homes, and she also celebrated her native heritage at a time when native Canadian culture was misunderstood and undervalued by many white Canadians.

Emily Pauline Johnson was born on the Six Nations Reserve near Brantford, Ontario. Her father, George Johnson, was a Mohawk chief; her mother, Emily Susanna, was white. Her parents had met at the home of an Anglican minister. George

Johnson acted as the minister's interpreter with native people on the reserve, and Emily, an Englishwoman, was visiting her sister, the minister's wife. The two fell in love and married, although both families were at first against the union. George Johnson moved with his bride into a beautiful mansion, called Chiefswood, on the banks of the Grand River. Eventually they became the parents of four children: two boys and two girls. Pauline was the youngest.

Pauline had a happy childhood, enjoying the cultural traditions of both her parents. Her mother taught her to enjoy the poetry of Shakespeare, Milton, and Keats. Pauline's Mohawk grandfather, John "Smoke" Johnson, spent many hours with his granddaughter, telling her native legends and traditions. Pauline loved to canoe on the Grand River and to wander in the forest near her home. By the time she was a teenager, Pauline had written many poems about nature or based on her grandfather's stories.

In 1884 Pauline Johnson's contented life at Chiefswood came to an abrupt end. Her father died of injuries that he suffered while trying to stop illegal lumber cutters on the reserve. The family could no longer afford to live in Chiefswood, so Pauline, her mother, and her sister, Eva, moved to a rented house in Brantford. Eva got a job in an office. Johnson looked for a way to earn money, too, and she began sending out her poems to newspapers and magazines. Her first sale was to the local newspaper, the *Brantford Expositor*.

A collection of poems by Canadian poets called *Songs of the Great Dominion,* which included two poems by Johnson, was sent to a reviewer for a British literary magazine. The reviewer praised Johnson's poems in the magazine, establishing her literary reputation in England. Although recognition of her work was growing, Johnson found that her earnings were meagre.

"The Song My Paddle Sings," one of her most famous poems, brought only $3 when first published in *Saturday Night* magazine. She had to earn more, but how?

In January 1892 Johnson, along with several other poets, was asked to read at a meeting of the Young Liberal Club of Toronto. Introduced as the "Indian Poet Princess," she gave a dramatic reading that was the hit of the evening and received glowing reviews in the Toronto newspapers. One journalist quickly arranged for Johnson to do another poetry evening all by herself. Next, he scheduled an ambitious series of 125 readings in Ontario and Quebec communities. Johnson's career as a performer was launched.

In the days before radio and television, people depended on travelling performers for entertainment—and Johnson found that she had a gift for performance, sometimes moving audiences to tears. In the early days, Johnson wore a simple white dress for her performances. But soon she developed a "Mohawk Princess" costume that she designed herself. The dress was made of fringed buckskin decorated with rabbit fur. She also wore a necklace of bear claws around her throat, beaded bracelets around her wrists, and moccasins on her feet. Johnson would appear in these clothes in the first half of her performance, reciting dramatic poems such as "The Song My Paddle Sings"—expressing native-Canadian themes. After an intermission, she would reappear in an evening dress and recite patriotic poems. In keeping with her dual heritage, she billed herself both as Pauline Johnson and with her great-grandfather's Mohawk name, Tekahionwake, which can be translated as "Double Life," a fitting name for her. In 1894 Johnson made a successful tour of England, and the following year, her first book of poetry, *The White Wampum,* was published. These poems were about native culture and the importance of preserving traditional beliefs.

In 1901 Johnson teamed up with another performer, Walter McRaye, who recited poems about Quebec. Together they toured Canada numerous times, as well as the United States, Europe, and Australia. In 1903 Johnson and McRaye made a trip along the Cariboo Road in British Columbia, which had once been a gold-rush route. They travelled up the steep trail in a surrey pulled by four horses. Native Canadians, ranchers, and miners travelled forty to fifty miles to Lac la Hache to see the poets' recital in a large barn. Johnson had to dress for her performance in an oat bin.

Johnson loved the Canadian West, and her travels inspired many of her poems. "Train Dogs" grew out of seeing an exhausted dogsled team and driver arrive in Edmonton. She wrote "The Riders of the Plains" about the North-West Mounted Police to defend them from criticism she heard from American friends.

In 1906 Johnson made a second triumphant tour of England. In London, she met Chief Joe Capilano from British Columbia. He was there to speak to the King and Queen on behalf of his Squamish people, who were in danger of losing their traditional hunting and fishing rights.

By 1909 Johnson felt exhausted by touring and she longed for a quiet life. She decided to settle in Vancouver, a place she had grown to love during her many visits there. She and Walter McRaye gave a farewell performance in Vancouver, and then McRaye continued on as a performer without her.

Now Johnson finally had time to collect her poems into one volume: *Flint and Feather*, published in 1912. She also wrote stories about native Canadian children, which were published in a children's magazine called *Boys' World*. Chief Joe Capilano, who had become a close friend, had told her many traditional tales of the Squamish people. She added some Iroquois stories from her childhood to the collection, which was published as *Legends of Vancouver* in 1911.

When Johnson finally consulted a doctor about her continuing exhaustion, she discovered that she had breast cancer, too far advanced to be treated. She died on March 7, 1913, just three days before her fifty-second birthday. Her funeral was attended by many Canadian leaders, both native and non-native. Her ashes were buried in Stanley Park—to this day, the only person ever to be buried there. In 1961, Canada Post issued a stamp to mark the one-hundredth anniversary of Pauline Johnson's birth. It was the first Canadian stamp to honour a native Canadian— and the first to honour a woman who was not a member of the royal family. Today, Johnson's birthplace, Chiefswood, is a national historic site and is open to the public.

# James Naismith
## 1861–1939

THE ORIGINS OF MOST TEAM SPORTS are mysterious. Historians still argue about when baseball began or where the first game of hockey was played. But there is no mystery about basketball. The game was introduced on December 21, 1891, and it was the invention of one man—James Naismith.

James Naismith was born in the small farming community of Bennie's Corners, near Almonte, Ontario. He was the eldest son of Scottish immigrants. Both his parents died in a typhoid epidemic when he was just ten years old, and he and his younger brother and older sister were then raised by a stern uncle. James received mediocre grades in the one-room schoolhouse he attended, but he was strong and energetic. He helped out on his uncle's farm after school, and he was the strongest swimmer and best hockey player among all his friends. Since he didn't want to ask his uncle to buy him skates, he made his own: two strips of wood with metal files set in them that he could attach to his regular boots.

To help out with money for the family, Naismith left school to work in a lumber camp, cutting trees and sawing logs. When he later returned to high school, he found that his mind was as agile as his body. Concentrating hard on his studies, he finished four years of high school in just a year and a half. Then, in 1883, he went on to McGill University in Montreal to take a four-year bachelor of arts program. He decided that he would spend all his time on his studies, until friends persuaded him that he would do better in class if he kept himself fit. He took up gymnastics and competed in the school rugby program. He did so well that in 1885 he was awarded a silver medal for best all-around athlete. He earned a gold medal in 1887. In that same year, he graduated from McGill, near the top of his class.

After graduation, Naismith began studies at a Presbyterian theological college. He also worked as the director of physical education at McGill. Although his instructors at the Presbyterian college frowned on rough contact sports as "tools of the devil," James continued to play lacrosse and rugby. He believed in the adage that a healthy body makes a healthy mind. Although he had strong religious beliefs, he was not sure that he wanted to become a minister. Then an incident made it clear to him what path he should follow. While he was on the rugby field one day, something went wrong in practice. The guard playing next to him began to swear loudly. Suddenly he stopped and turned to Naismith saying, "I beg your pardon, Jim. I didn't notice you were there."

"I hadn't paid particular attention," Naismith would later recall, "for I had heard more fluent swearing than that in the lumber camps." Still, the incident started him thinking about how he could be a good influence on young people through sports. The YMCA (Young Men's Christian Association) had been formed in Montreal back in 1851, and Naismith often visited the athletic club during his school days. He discussed his thoughts with the general secretary of the YMCA, who suggested that he attend the organization's International Training School in Springfield, Massachusetts. At the YMCA Training School (later called Springfield College), he could take courses that emphasized both physical and spiritual development.

It was now late summer of 1890 and Naismith, almost thirty, was one of the oldest students at the YMCA school. The following year he became an instructor of physical education at the college. In the fall of 1891, he was given a special teaching assignment. Luther Gulick, head of the physical education department, had been having a difficult time motivating students to stay fit during the winter. All the school offered were monotonous exercise routines. Gulick challenged Naismith to come up with an enjoyable indoor game that students could learn quickly.

At first, Naismith tried to modify various outdoor games like soccer, rugby, and lacrosse so they could be played in the gymnasium, but none of them worked well. Then Naismith remembered a rock-throwing game he had played with his boyhood friends. His new game, he decided, should involve throwing a ball at some sort of target. The ball must be big enough (but not too heavy) to be caught and thrown easily. If the target was raised, the attempts to hit it with the ball would favour skill over strength. To avoid injuries on the hard wooden floors, no one would be permitted to run with the ball, and aggressive body contact would not be allowed. On December 21, 1891, Naismith posted the original thirteen rules of his new game on the school bulletin board. Some of the rules would later change—there was no dribbling at first; the ball could be advanced only by passing it. However, the basics of the game Naismith came up with have remained essentially the same for more than 110 years.

To play the first game, James Naismith divided his class of eighteen students into two teams of nine. He used two peach baskets for his targets, attached to the edge of a balcony 3 metres above the gymnasium floor. In the early games, the bottoms of the baskets weren't cut out, so someone had to climb a ladder to get the ball out. The first game moved slowly as the players struggled to remember the rules. The final score was 1–0 (a far cry from the games of today!) but Naismith's invention was a success.

Word of Naismith's new indoor game spread with amazing speed. Students began telling their friends about it during the Christmas break from school, and by January of 1892 the rules were printed in a YMCA magazine called *The Triangle*. Some people wanted to call the new game Naismith Ball, but the ever-modest inventor preferred the name Basket Ball, which eventually became basketball.

Like Naismith, five of the eighteen players at the Springfield school were from Canada, and they helped spread the popularity of basketball back home. The game was introduced in France by 1893, and was demonstrated in England in 1894. By 1901, basketball was being played all over the world, though it would always enjoy its greatest popularity in the land of its invention—the United States. The first international tournament was held when the Americans hosted the 1904 Olympics in St. Louis, though basketball did not become an official Olympic sport until 1936.

Naismith became famous as the inventor of basketball, and though he never sought publicity for it, he was on hand to be honoured at the 1936 Berlin Olympics. He was seventy-four years old by then, and nearing the end of his long teaching career. Naismith had remained at the Springfield YMCA Training School until 1895, when he moved to Denver to become director of physical education at the YMCA there. He also studied medicine at the University of Colorado and graduated as a doctor in 1898. He later served as a doctor, a professor, a Presbyterian minister, and the director of physical education at the University of Kansas. He remained at the school until 1937, when he was given the honorary position of professor emeritus and retired. He died in 1939.

Two years after his death, the Naismith Memorial Basketball Hall of Fame was organized in Springfield, Massachusetts. Though it would take several years to get the project off the ground, James Naismith himself was among the group of people selected when the Basketball Hall of Fame finally inducted its first members in 1959. Naismith was honoured by his native Canada in 1991, with a postage stamp commemorating the 100th anniversary of basketball.

# Martha Black
## 1866–1957

"**G**OLD, GOLD, GOLD—A TON OF GOLD,"
trumpeted the headlines. Gold had been discovered in the Klondike region of the Yukon,
and in the summer of 1897, newspapers were spreading the word.
All over North America, people read the stories and dreamed of
striking it rich. Among them was Martha Louise Purdy of Chicago.

At thirty-one, Martha Purdy had a wealthy husband, two
children, and a beautiful home. But she gave up this settled
and comfortable life to follow the lure of gold. She began the
journey to the Klondike with a party of men that included her
husband, Will Purdy, and her brother, George Munger. Will

Purdy backed out of the expedition when they reached Seattle (in 1898), but Martha was determined to carry on. She had finally broken away from a life that was stifling her, and she would not turn back. She never saw Will again.

To get to the goldfields, the greatest barrier was the steep, treacherous Chilkoot Pass. Martha never forgot the anguish of the climb, hampered by the corsets, the long, dragging skirt, and the dainty leather boots that women then wore. She used spruce roots and jagged rocks to haul herself up, slipping on patches of snow that still clung to the trail, even in summer, stumbling and sometimes crawling. Her brother urged her on: "Buck up and be a man!" he shouted. "Show some style!" His words gave her the angry energy she needed to drag herself up the last 30 metres. Still ahead was an 800-kilometre journey down the Yukon River, to reach Dawson City. By then, Martha realized that, before parting from her husband, she had become pregnant.

Dawson City had sprung up quickly, becoming the largest Canadian community west of Winnipeg. It was a raw, bustling town of shacks and tents when Martha arrived. The buildings still smelled of new lumber, and the muddy streets were choked with thousands of gold seekers and their gear. Martha and George found a cabin on a hill overlooking the town. There, in January 1899, while George was away in the goldfields, she gave birth to a son, alone in the cabin. Fortunately, it was an easy delivery. The community was thrilled by the new arrival, and even rough and rugged prospectors flocked to the cabin to see the baby. Martha always remembered that one of the men had a hook in place of his missing hand, which he wrapped in soft cotton so that he could safely handle the baby.

In the spring of 1899 a major gold discovery was made in Nome, Alaska, and within a week, Dawson lost half its population as the gold seekers moved on. But Martha intended to stay.

She had fallen in love with the wild natural beauty of the Yukon: "its stark and splendid mountains; its lordly Yukon River; its midnight sun," as she described it. The claim Martha had staked at Excelsior Creek was producing gold, and she opened a sawmill, which also became very successful. By the early 1900s she had divorced her husband and brought her two older children to live with her in Dawson.

When Martha needed a lawyer for some company business, a friend recommended George Black. Within two weeks of meeting her, George proposed, but Martha took two years to say yes. The couple were married in 1904, and in 1905 George Black was elected to the Yukon Council. In 1912 he was appointed commissioner of the Yukon Territory. Martha welcomed all Yukoners to Government House, calling it "the house of the people," which should be open to "all who wished to come, irrespective of social position." She had always loved flowers and she planned the Government House gardens.

In 1916 George resigned as commissioner to organize the Yukon Infantry Company to fight in the First World War. When his unit went overseas, Martha insisted on going along. While George fought in France, Martha stayed in England, serving as a war correspondent for the *Dawson City News* and *Whitehorse Star*. She also gave nearly 400 public lectures about the natural wonders of the Yukon, for which she was made a Fellow of the Royal Geographic Society.

In 1925 George was elected as the Member of Parliament for the Yukon. When he had to resign because of ill health in 1935, Martha ran in his place, campaigning across his vast Yukon constituency. She later recalled some hecklers who asked what an old woman could do for them in Ottawa. Martha retorted, "You'll be lucky when you reach my age if you have my sturdy legs, my good stomach, my strong heart, and what I like to call my headpiece." Although the Liberals won the election nationally, Martha, a Conservative, held onto the Yukon seat. At the age of sixty-nine, she became the second woman to sit in the House of Commons, joining Agnes Macphail. As an MP, she was particularly interested in issues related to public health, pensions, and unemployment, as well as nature conservation.

Despite her many accomplishments, Martha had traditional views about her role as George's wife. She wrote in her diary that she felt George made a far better Member of Parliament than she did. In her view, she was simply holding his seat for him until he was well enough to take it back. In 1940 George did regain the seat, and held it until 1949.

Martha wrote two books, one about Yukon flowers and a memoir of her eventful life called *My Seventy Years*. Martha Black died in Whitehorse at the age of ninety-one. George lived on until 1965, when he was ninety-four. Both Blacks were beloved in the Yukon, and honours were showered on them during their lives and after. In 1997 Canada Post issued a stamp honouring Martha Louise Black.

# Reginald Fessenden
## 1866–1932

I N 1876, when Reginald Fessenden was only ten years old, he watched Alexander Graham Bell demonstrate his telephone in his lab in Brantford, Ontario. Six days later, Bell would make the first long-distance call in history. (See Alexander Graham Bell's biography for more about this invention.) From then on, an idea was buzzing around in the boy's head: could voices be transmitted *without* wires? He thought there must be a way to do it. Ten years later, working for inventor Thomas Alva Edison, Fessenden shared his dream of broadcasting voices. Edison was not encouraging. "Fezzie, what do you say are man's chances of jumping over the moon?" the great inventor asked. "I think one is as likely as the other." Which shows that even great inventors can be short-sighted. In 1900 Fessenden's own voice would be the first ever transmitted by radio waves and heard by another person. But he would struggle all his life to get recognition for his achievements.

Ronald Fessenden was born in East Bolton, Quebec, the son of an Anglican minister. The family moved several times, as his father took up new parishes. Fessenden spent part of his childhood in Fergus, Ontario, and part in Niagara Falls. He was a brilliant student, and at age fourteen, won a mathematics mastership (like a scholarship) to Bishop's College in Lennoxville, Quebec. This gave him a small income and credit for a college year if he passed their exams, which he did. When he was eighteen, however, the restless Fessenden left his studies without getting a degree. He accepted a teaching position in Bermuda. While there, he met his future wife, Helen.

The couple soon returned to North America so that Fessenden could apply for a job with Thomas Edison—the inventor he most admired—at his machine shop in New York. Fessenden was first hired as an instrument tester, but was eventually promoted to Edison's lab as chief chemist. He was only twenty-four years old.

Unfortunately, Edison had financial problems which forced him to let Fessenden go. Fessenden then went to work for George Westinghouse and helped design the electrical lighting for the 1893 Columbian Exposition (a forerunner of modern World's Fairs) in Chicago. Next, he went on to become a professor of electrical engineering at Purdue University in Indiana and, later, Western University of Pennsylvania in Pittsburgh. During these years, Fessenden was able to continue his work on transmitting sound without wires.

In 1901 Guglielmo Marconi startled the world by sending a radio signal from Cornwall, England, to Signal Hill in

Newfoundland. It was the Morse Code message for the letter *s*: three faint, short beeps. For this he has always been known as the Father of Radio. Yet the much less famous Fessenden had a strong claim for the title, too. Marconi was mainly interested in sending Morse Code; Fessenden wanted to transmit the human voice and music.

Fessenden believed that radio waves rippled outward from a point, like waves when a stone is thrown into water. He had come up with the theory of the "continuous wave": a way to allow sound to "ride" on these rippling radio waves. A generator could transmit the radio waves to a receiver. The receiver would then remove the radio waves and leave the listener with the sound. Fessenden's theory was correct. However, Marconi had put forward a different theory, and Marconi's work was better funded than Fessenden's. Marconi also had an ease and charm in dealing with the press and public that the shy and prickly Fessenden lacked. For at least ten years, Marconi's ideas were accepted and Fessenden's were ignored.

In 1900 Fessenden went to work for the U.S. Weather Bureau, which was interested in finding better ways to transmit weather reports. On December 23, standing on an island in the middle of the Potomac River near Washington, D.C., Fessenden spoke these words: "One, two, three, four. Is it snowing where you are, Mr. Thiessen? If it is, would you telegraph back to me?" Mr. Thiessen, 1 kilometre away, confirmed he had heard the message. This was the first radio transmission of the human voice—a year before Marconi's more celebrated achievement. In 1902, though, Fessenden's work with the bureau came to an end, in a squabble over whether Fessenden or the U.S. Weather Bureau should own rights to his new invention.

With the backing of two Philadelphia millionaires, Fessenden formed the National Electric Signaling Company

(NESCO). This arrangement allowed Fessenden to continue his work and build more powerful generators to transmit radio signals. In 1903 he sent a voice message 80 kilometres. He established wireless stations in the United States and on ships belonging to the United Fruit Company. But Fessenden had still made only point-to-point transmissions involving one speaker and one listener. His most spectacular achievement came on Christmas Eve 1906.

Wireless operators using NESCO radios on United Fruit Company ships in Boston Harbor and out in the Atlantic had been alerted to stand by for something special. Normally, their radios emitted only the measured beeps of Morse Code. But to their amazement, they heard Fessenden's voice. He made a short speech, played "O Holy Night" on his violin, then Helen and a friend sang some Christmas carols. This was the first broadcast— voice and music transmissions heard in several locations at once.

Fessenden continued perfecting radio transmissions. Once again, though, there were disagreements between Fessenden and his backers. They could see no future in voice broadcasting. Morse Code seemed far more practical. They tried to break off their association with Fessenden and seize his patents. This time, Fessenden sued them to get back the rights to his work.

To earn a living while the lawsuit dragged on, Fessenden continued to work on other inventions. In his lifetime, he patented over 200 different inventions. One was an early version of microfilm. Another was an early form of sonar, which Fessenden called the Fathometer. Its original function was to measure the depth of water under a ship by bouncing sound waves off the bottom. Eventually it was put to military use in detecting enemy submarines.

In the 1920s Fessenden was finally recognized by his peers for his pioneer work in radio, although his name never became well known. The NESCO lawsuit was at long last settled out of court in 1928, and Fessenden, ill and exhausted, retired to Bermuda. He died there, a nearly forgotten man, in his house by the sea. His memorial stone in Bermuda bears the words "His mind illuminated the past and the future." Today Fessenden is given credit for the theories that led to all later radio and television transmissions.

# Maude Abbott
## 1869–1940

**M**AUDE ABBOTT was a pioneering physician, medical historian, and teacher who became a world authority on heart diseases. Yet her life began in tragedy and she encountered many difficulties along the way.

Maude was born in St. Andrews East, Quebec. Her father, Jeremiah Babin, was an Anglican minister. Her mother, Elizabeth Abbott, was a member of a respectable family that included a future prime minister of Canada. However, two years before Maude's birth, her father had been accused of murdering his sister. Although he was found not guilty, many people in his community did not accept the verdict. He fled before Maude was born, and her mother died of tuberculosis seven months after giving birth to Maude.

Fortunately for Maude and her older sister, Alice, her widowed grandmother, Frances Mary Abbott, adopted the girls and gave them a loving home. Frances Abbott was a lively and intelligent woman who believed that her grandchildren should receive a good education. She hired a tutor for them, but Maude longed to go to school and mingle with other young people. Finally she got her wish in 1894, when she was fifteen. Her grandmother enrolled her in a private girls school in Montreal. Maude Abbott was an outstanding student and received a scholarship to begin an arts degree at McGill University.

McGill had only begun admitting women students two years before Abbott applied, and there were still very few women studying there. Once again, Abbott did very well in her studies. She was also active in a women's debating society and became one of the editors of McGill's student newspaper. At her graduation in 1890, she was both a medal winner and class valedictorian—the student chosen to deliver an address to the graduating class. By now, Abbott had become more interested in science and laboratory work. For a long time, she had been thinking about studying medicine, but this was still a very unusual path for a woman to take. "May I be a doctor?" she asked her grandmother. "Dear child," said her grandmother, at a time when few people would have been so encouraging to a young woman, "you may be anything you like."

But McGill University was not as advanced in its thinking. Abbott applied to the medical faculty in the fall of 1889. After delaying their reply for months, the faculty informed her that, as a woman, she could not be admitted. Abbott did not give up. Several of her women friends were also determined to study medicine. They formed the Association for the Promotion of

Professional Education for Women and petitioned McGill University to reconsider. The Montreal *Gazette* newspaper supported them. At this point, a group of prominent physicians in Montreal spoke out against medical studies for women. They argued that women lacked the necessary stamina; their nerves were too weak; they would lose their "maidenly modesty" by studying the human body; and anyway, their place was in the home. Once again, McGill refused to admit women to the medical school.

There was another medical school in Montreal, at Bishop's College. It did not have McGill's splendid facilities, but it was much more open in its admissions policy. The Bishop's medical school had admitted both black and Jewish students at a time when other Canadian medical schools were discriminating against them. The medical faculty sent a letter to Abbott inviting her to attend, and she accepted. Yet prejudice against women continued to make her studies difficult.

All medical students needed to do clinical work at Montreal General Hospital, which had close ties with the medical school at McGill. To be admitted to the hospital wards, medical students had to purchase an admission ticket. Abbott sent money to the hospital for her ticket as soon as she entered medical school. By the time her second year began and she was ready to begin hospital rounds, the hospital still had not given her a ticket. After her struggle was reported in the newspapers, some of the hospital's governors took Abbott's side. They threatened to cut off their charitable donations to the hospital. Only then did the Montreal General give in and grant Abbott her ticket. She received her medical diploma in 1894, winning the prize for anatomy and another prize for the highest marks on her final examinations.

For the next three years, Maude Abbott, accompanied by her sister, Alice, studied in Europe. In Switzerland, and especially in

Vienna, Austria, she studied internal medicine and pathology (the study of disease) with some of the greatest medical figures of her time. She also collected and preserved lab specimens of unusual medical conditions that she would later put to great use in teaching medicine. Alice Abbott had been studying music in Europe, but she began to suffer from a mental illness that produced extreme mood swings. At that time, there was no effective treatment for the condition, and for many years Maude searched for a cure for her sister. Grandmother Abbott had died in 1890, so Maude Abbott was solely responsible for Alice's care for the rest of her life.

In 1897, when Abbott first returned to Canada, she opened a clinic for women and children in Montreal; however, her first love was research. She wrote an important paper on heart murmurs, based on her studies in Europe, but a male friend had to present it for her. Women were not admitted to the Montreal Medical Society where the paper was to be read.

In 1898, to her great happiness, Abbott was hired by the McGill Faculty of Medicine as the assistant curator of the pathology museum. (In 1901, she would become the curator, a position she held until 1936.) In the days before colour photographs and other teaching aids, specimens were very important in the teaching of medicine. Yet, when Abbott took over the museum, it was almost useless for study. There was no classification system for the specimens; some had no proper identifying labels. Abbott painstakingly put them in order, creating a classification system that was later used by medical museums around the world. She catalogued thousands of specimens, and used them in the pathology classes she taught.

In 1906 Abbott wrote a paper about congenital heart problems. (A congenital problem is one you're born with.) Her thorough study was based on more than 400 cases. Dr. William

Osler, one of the world's most renowned doctors, included it as a chapter in his classic textbook, *System of Modern Medicine*. He wrote to her about her chapter: "It is by far the best thing ever written on the subject in English, possibly in any language. For years it will be the standard work on the subject." This work, and Osler's admiration, established her as a world authority on the heart.

Maude Abbott felt a strong attachment to McGill University throughout her career. Hard work and the quest for knowledge were the most important things to her. However, she did, from time to time, request salary increases or promotions, since money was always a problem, with Alice to care for. Almost always, she was turned down. From our viewpoint today, it is painfully clear how grudging McGill was in recognizing her brilliance. After Abbott had a worldwide reputation, McGill made her a lecturer in pathology—the lowliest academic ranking. She never advanced beyond the position of assistant professor in her entire career. There is little doubt that a man with the same credentials would have been a full professor.

Although she did not have the academic position (or the salary) that she deserved, many doctors did value her knowledge. Young cardiologists came from all over the United States and Europe to study with this world-renowned pathologist. She was welcomed at conferences, and she gave guest lectures throughout Europe and North America. Her huge work, *Atlas of Congenital Cardiac Disease*, was published in 1936, the year she retired from McGill. The book described more than a thousand cases. In the decades ahead, doctors were able to save thousands of "blue babies"—babies born with blue-tinged skin because their hearts were damaged—because of Abbott's studies.

During her lifetime, Abbott wrote over 140 medical papers. And that was just a small part of her workload. She would never say no to a project that helped doctors to share information. From 1907 until 1938, she was the international secretary and editor of the *Journal of the International Association of Medical Museums*. She was also an editor of the *Journal of the Canadian Medical Association*. She helped to found the International Association of Medical Museums in 1907 and was one of the founders of the Federation of Medical Women of Canada in 1924. This latter group began with just six members but today has more than two thousand.

Abbott died of a stroke at the age of seventy-one. Upon her death, medical journals were filled with outpourings of respect and affection from eminent doctors who had known her. On March 10, 2000, a crowd of doctors and dignitaries filled the Osler Library at McGill University. Cabinet Minister Lucienne Robillard unveiled a brass plaque and oil portrait of Maude Abbott, who had done so much to advance medical knowledge and to lead the way for women in medicine.

# Stephen Leacock

## 1869–1944

STEPHEN LEACOCK is one of Canada's most beloved humorists, and is still, a half-century after his death, one of our most popular writers. His books have been translated into many languages, making people laugh all over the world.

Stephen Butler Leacock was born in Hampshire, England, near the village of Swanmore. His father, Walter Peter, came from a wealthy family, but had been banished for marrying, at the age of eighteen, without his parents' permission. Walter Peter had few practical skills: he tried farming in South Africa; then the Leacocks returned for a few years to England, where he worked as an asphalt contractor. Stephen, the third of the Leacock children, was born there. After another failed farming venture, this time in the United States, the Leacocks staked their future on a 100-acre farm near the town of Sutton, Ontario, not far from Lake Simcoe.

As Stephen Leacock described it later, in his whimsical way, "My parents migrated to Canada in 1876, and I decided to go with them"—he was then six years old. Despite the humour he found in it afterwards, he was facing some difficult years. The family eventually grew to eleven children, and their father still had no inclination to work hard to support them. The farmhouse was shabby and poorly heated, and the older children had to help out with back-breaking chores. It was Stephen's academic brilliance that saved him from the drudgery of the farm. His wealthy grandfather sent money from England so that he could attend Upper Canada College in Toronto, where Leacock became co-editor of the school paper and graduated as Head Boy in 1887.

Leacock went on to the University of Toronto, but after one year he had to leave. He became a high-school teacher in small Ontario towns, to help his mother and eight younger brothers and sisters still at home. (His father had now left his family, and Leacock would never see him again.) To make extra money, he began to write humorous pieces for magazines in Canada and the United States.

When Leacock was hired as a teacher at his old school, Upper Canada College, he was finally able to complete his degree at the University of Toronto as a part-time student. Then he went on to graduate work in political economy at the University of Chicago.

For Stephen Leacock, the first years of the twentieth century were filled with happiness and success. In 1900 he married

Beatrix (Trix) Hamilton, and a year later he started a teaching career, at McGill University in Montreal, that would last for the next thirty-six years. In 1906 he had his first book published, a university textbook called *Elements of Political Science*. It was this book, not any of his humorous story collections, which earned Leacock the most money during his lifetime. It was eventually translated into nineteen languages and was required reading in many North American universities. Leacock had become a popular and respected professor at McGill, and in 1908 he was appointed head of the Department of Political Science and Economics. By then, he was also a sought-after guest lecturer in England and other countries.

The Leacocks purchased some property on the shores of Lake Couchiching in Orillia, Ontario, and began to spend every summer there. Leacock became a star player for the local cricket club and sailed on the lake, but he also spent every morning working on his stories. In 1910, with his own money, he published *Literary Lapses*—a collection of the funny pieces he had written over the previous decade. The book included one of Leacock's best-loved stories, "My Financial Career," about a timid man trying to open a bank account. The book was an immediate success, and publishers approached him, begging for more. Leacock now had a choice of two very promising careers: as an academic or as a humour writer. He decided to continue with both.

His next book was *Nonsense Novels*, which made fun of the popular fiction of his day. For instance, "Gertrude the Governess" had a reckless romantic hero who "flung himself from the room, flung himself upon his horse, and rode madly off in all directions."

In 1912 Leacock published his comic masterpiece, *Sunshine Sketches of a Little Town*, with Orillia thinly disguised as the town of Mariposa. Although the satire was gentle, some people in Orillia felt embarrassed, even indignant, about being recognizable figures in his book. Over the years, however, Orillia came to be proud of its best-known resident. Leacock was now a famous and financially secure man. He and Trix bought a large and elegant house in Montreal, where they spent the school year, and in August of 1912, their only child, also named Stephen, was born.

Leacock was working harder than ever, going on frequent speaking tours and turning out book after book. In all, he produced some sixty books in his career, evenly divided between works about politics, economics, and history, and the humorous books for which he is best known today. He also continued to write articles for American, British, and Canadian newspapers and magazines. In 1921 he helped to found the Canadian Authors Association.

Trix died of cancer in 1925. Leacock grieved deeply, but kept busy with his writing and a new enthusiasm: he was planning the house he had always dreamed of for his lakeside property in Orillia. The house, which he called "Old Brewery Bay," was completed in 1928 and became a happy gathering place for relatives and friends. As soon as spring term ended at McGill University, Leacock came up to Orillia in a motorcade, bringing supplies, housekeeping staff, and his niece Barbara, who served as his secretary. As always, mornings were for work, but afternoons were for spending time with his son, fishing, and gardening.

By the end of the 1935–1936 school year, Leacock had passed the age when all McGill professors were forced to retire. He fought against the ruling, but McGill would not give in. Other universities were eager to hire him, but he decided to concentrate on his writing instead. He went on his last speaking tour in the fall of 1936, through Canada's West. His book based on that tour, *My Discovery of the West,* won the Governor General's Award for Literature in 1937.

Stephen Leacock continued writing until his death in 1944. Within days of his passing, a committee formed by his friends had come up with fitting ways to honour him. Among other things, they established the Stephen Leacock Medal for Humour, to be awarded annually to the outstanding book of Canadian humour. First given in 1947, the award is still made every year. Leacock's name was also given to a building at McGill University and a mountain in Yukon's Saint Elias range. In 1969 a six-cent postage stamp was issued in his honour. Stephen Leacock's home in Orillia is now a national historic site and a public museum.

# R.B. Bennett
## 1870–1947

RICHARD BEDFORD BENNETT was born in Hopewell Hill, New Brunswick. Even as a boy, he had big dreams. He told his friends that he would grow up to be prime minister, and he spent much of his time reading books and practising speeches. Still, very little in his young life gave any hint of what was to come.

Bennett's father, Henry, had inherited the family's ship-building business at nearby Hopewell Cape, but by the 1870s the era of wooden ships was almost over. The Bennetts were forced to live on their savings and tend to their small farm. When Henry Bennett became an alcoholic and lost his business,

Richard's mother poured all her hopes into her five children.

Young Richard helped his mother with the chores around the house and on the farm. He also worked hard at school and often went over his studies with his mother. Richard was a fast learner and he had an excellent memory. By the age of twelve he had completed grade 8 at the local elementary school. By the time he was sixteen, he had graduated from the provincial Normal School (a school for training teachers) with a first-class teaching licence.

R.B. Bennett, as he would come to be known, got his first job as a teacher in a small town outside of Moncton, New Brunswick. The job paid $160 per year. Two years later he became principal at Douglastown on the Miramichi River; he was now responsible for running three schools and was paid $500 per year.

While working as a principal in Douglastown, Bennett met several people in nearby Chatham, New Brunswick, who would play important roles in his life. One was a boy named Max Aitken, who would grow up to become Lord Beaverbrook. Another was Jennie Shirreff, who would marry lumber millionaire E.B. Eddy. Aitken would later run some of Bennett's first political campaigns, and both he and Shirreff would help Bennett become a rich man. Still, it was another man he met in Chatham who gave Bennett his start.

Lemuel J. Tweedie was a prominent New Brunswick lawyer who later became leader of the provincial Conservative Party. He offered Bennett a position as a clerk in his law office, and in 1890 Bennett left his principal's job to study law at Dalhousie University. Three years later, he graduated and became a lawyer in Tweedie's firm. In 1896 Bennett was elected to the town council in Chatham, but later that year he was offered the chance to go to Calgary as the partner of James Lougheed, one of the busiest lawyers in Western Canada and an important Conservative senator. Bennett left for Calgary in January of 1897.

In 1898 Bennett was elected to the Assembly of the Northwest Territories (which then included Alberta, not yet a province). Two years later, he ran as a Conservative in the federal election of 1900 but lost. After Alberta became a province in 1905, Bennett lost again when he tried to win a seat in the new Provincial Assembly. Still, his legal business prospered. James Lougheed had been the lawyer for the Canadian Pacific Railway and the Hudson's Bay Company. As Bennett took over more and more of Lougheed's legal responsibilities, he became the top lawyer for the CPR. By 1910 that job alone was paying him $10,000. With help from Max Aitken, Bennett invested his money wisely. By 1914 his total income was about $65,000 per year—equal in today's purchasing power to over $1 million. (In 1914 a skilled worker in Calgary could live reasonably well on about $3 per day.)

Bennett had returned to politics in 1909, and in the federal election of 1911 he won the riding of Calgary. Prime Minister Robert Borden gave him several important jobs to do, but Bennett was disappointed that he was not given a cabinet position as the head of one of the government ministries. He decided not to run for re-election in 1917. After Borden retired in 1920, the new prime minister, Arthur Meighen, asked Bennett to become his minister of finance. However, Meighen's Conservatives lost to the Liberals in 1921, and William Lyon Mackenzie King became prime minister.

After the Conservatives lost another election in 1926, the Party decided it was time for a new leader. In the past, only those elected to Parliament in Ottawa had chosen the leader. In 1927 it was decided to hold a meeting of all Conservative members— the first Conservative leadership convention. Bennett won the job, and in 1930 he led the Conservative Party to an election victory over King's Liberals. Now sixty years old, R.B. Bennett was the prime minister of Canada, but he had been elected at a very difficult time.

In late October of 1929, the industrialized world was plunged into a steep economic decline. In his election campaign speeches, Bennett had promised to improve Canadian unemployment problems. Once elected, his government spent $20 million on an Unemployment Relief Act. He also raised tariffs. This made products from other countries more costly, but Bennett hoped it would spur Canadians to buy Canadian goods and therefore help the Canadian economy. But no one had any idea how grim the Great Depression was to become.

All of Canada suffered during the Depression, but the Prairie provinces were hurt worst of all. Prairie farmers depended on the sale of wheat to survive; however, other countries could no longer afford to pay for Canadian wheat. Then a drought settled on the Prairies, making it impossible for farmers to grow their crops. In July of 1931, an Unemployment and Farm Relief Bill was introduced. It was extended in 1932, but conditions got worse. Farmers who could no longer afford to buy gasoline hitched horses to their cars, and these vehicles became known as "Bennett Buggies."

As the Great Depression got worse and worse, Bennett's leadership style made him appear like the man to blame. In addition to being prime minister, he had given himself four other ministries to run. Someone saw him talking to himself as he made his way down a corridor and said, only half-jokingly, "There's R.B. Bennett holding a Cabinet meeting." There were also complaints that Bennett was out of touch with the average person because he was a millionaire who wore fancy suits and a top hat and lived in a suite at Ottawa's elegant Chateau Laurier Hotel.

Because Bennett was prime minister, and because he was rich, people wrote to him asking for help. He received hundreds of despairing letters: from men who could not find work, from women who could not afford to feed their children, from families who might lose their houses because they could not pay their mortgages. Bennett or his secretary answered them all, and he usually included a small gift of money. He routinely gave thousands of dollars to charity. He never married or had children of his own, but at one time he was helping to support the education of eighteen young people.

The fall and winter of 1932–33 were the most desperate times of the Depression. Thousands of young men were out of work. At the suggestion of General Andrew McNaughton, the army offered to set up camps and work projects where the unemployed "would find a bed, food, clothing and medical treatment and be given work to build up their morale." Bennett liked the idea, and the camps helped . . . for a while.

By 1935 the economy was finally beginning to recover, and yet there were still tens of thousands of unemployed workers. Conservative policies had always been against government interference in business and social issues, but party popularity was fading badly. Influenced by American President Franklin Roosevelt and his "New Deal," Bennett proposed a new policy. He created the Canadian Wheat Board, to help control prices, and the Bank of Canada, to control interest rates. The Conservatives also passed laws providing minimum wages and unemployment insurance, as well as other social reforms. Given time, all these policies might have helped, but people were getting tired of Bennett's government. Then, in the early summer of 1935, men from the unemployment camps out West planned a "March on Ottawa." When a riot broke out after police stopped the marchers in Regina, people saw this as proof that the

Conservatives really did not care enough about labour issues. In the federal election that October, the Liberal slogan was "King or Chaos." The Liberals won in a landslide.

Bennett stayed on as leader of the Conservative Party until the summer of 1938. He was unhappy with the way his political career had turned out, and he moved to England in 1939. There, he was given the title of Viscount, and in 1941 he served the British government in the House of Lords. R.B. Bennett passed away on June 26, 1947. He was buried near his English estate in Surrey. He is the only Canadian prime minister not buried in Canada.

# Emily Carr
## 1871–1945

**" I** COULD NOT PAINT IN THE OLD WAY," Emily Carr
once wrote. "It is dead—meaningless—empty." Her
strong views on art kept her in poverty for many years.
The public, and even her own family, scorned her bold brush
strokes and simple shapes. But within her lifetime, her genius
was finally recognized. Today she is one of the most admired
Canadian artists.

Emily Carr was born in Victoria, British Columbia, the
youngest of five daughters. (A brother came along later.) Her
parents were recent immigrants from England, and her father
was a prosperous merchant. The family lived in a fine, large

house on ten acres of land. Emily should have had a carefree early childhood, but she was always the child who didn't fit in. The English community in Victoria was prim and proper, and Emily was a noisy, rebellious child who liked to be active and get dirty.

When Emily was twelve, her much-loved mother died, followed by her father two years later. She came under the care of her stern eldest sister, Edith, who was determined to make Emily into a proper young lady. Instead, Emily withdrew from the family, riding her pony and spending hours drawing. In 1890, after her sister had slapped her until she fainted, Emily Carr left home to pursue her dream of studying art in San Francisco. She was nineteen.

The San Francisco School of Art was a shock to Emily. It was housed in a hall above a large market in an old part of the city. As the students worked, rats scuttled to and fro across the floor. But Carr was learning to paint, even though she clashed often with her instructors. She stayed at the school for five years, boarding with family friends.

When she returned home, Carr started children's art classes. At first she held the classes in the house, but her older sisters objected to the mess. So Carr converted the loft of their cow barn into a studio. The family gardener helped her by cutting a big hole in the roof and fitting glass into it, for a skylight. Even though the studio was plain and the roof leaked when it rained, Carr loved it: it was the first workspace that she could call her own. That summer, Carr took a trip that changed her life. She visited family friends who were Christian missionaries in the small, native Canadian village of Ucluelet, on the west coast of Vancouver Island. She was impressed by the way the Nuu-chah-nulth people seemed to live in harmony with nature, instead of trying to tame it and change it the way the gardeners of Victoria did.

When Carr had enough money saved from her children's art classes, she boarded a ship to England for further art studies. The great city of London, which she had heard so much about from her parents, was a disappointment to her. After British Columbia, it seemed grimy and overcrowded. Her favourite place was Kew Gardens, where she could stroll in a grove of trees that included some Canadian maples.

When she had been studying in London for a year, her favourite sister, Alice, came over for a visit. They enjoyed sightseeing together, but Carr was hurt when it became obvious that her sister was unimpressed by her drawings. Carr made a vow that she would never again show that she cared what people thought of her art. While she was in London, she had a marriage proposal from a Victoria friend who had come over to visit her. She decided that, although she liked him very much, she did not love him; and besides, she wanted to devote her life to art, not to marriage and family life. After her suitor went home, she studied and painted such long hours that her health broke down. Her sister Lizzie came to England to bring her back to Victoria. Carr was now thirty-three years old and felt that she had so far achieved nothing.

Emily moved to Vancouver in 1905, and as she got her strength back, she planned a new way to live. She would teach art to children in the winter, and in the summer she would travel the seacoast of British Columbia. She would explore the ancient and abandoned native villages, with their leaning and fallen totem poles. And she would paint them.

For four summers, Carr travelled along the coasts of Vancouver Island, to Haida Gwaii (the Queen Charlotte Islands) and the Gitxsan lands on the mainland near the Skeena River, recording a vanishing way of life. She begged rides from fishermen to take her along the coast with them; then she would hitch rides on passing wagons to get where she wanted to go. She took only her dog for company. She slept in tool sheds, tents, and the homes of native people.

Yet Carr was still unsatisfied with the painting techniques she had learned in art school. They didn't give her the tools she needed to paint the vibrant and mysterious natural world she saw on her journeys. By 1910 she had saved enough money to go to France to see the art of the Impressionists. Emily was inspired by their work. She took more art classes in France, but, as always, she found that her teachers took her work less seriously because she was a woman. She enjoyed herself more while painting for several months in the French countryside.

Then, once again, Carr returned to Victoria. Unable to pay city taxes on their large family property, the Carr sisters sold off most of it, and divided the rest among themselves. (Their sickly brother had died young.) In her mid-forties, Emily Carr built an apartment building on her piece of land, which she called "the House of All Sorts." Her plan was to rent out three apartments and use the fourth for her home and studio. However, things did not turn out as she had hoped. Her rents were not high enough to pay for a caretaker, so she had to do all the repairs herself. Furthermore, her paintings were not selling and no one wanted to take art lessons from her.

To the people of Victoria, Carr seemed wildly eccentric. She smoked at a time when this was not acceptable for ladies, and when she went downtown, she sometimes took along her pet monkey, Woo, wheeled in a baby carriage. Carr was also outspoken to the point of rudeness. She often quarrelled with her tenants and once, during an argument, hit one of them over the head with a pot. Desperate to earn some money, Carr turned to pottery and weaving, and here, finally, she had some success. She also bred and sold bobtail sheepdogs. But for fifteen years, caught up with all these money-making schemes, she did no painting.

There were, however, a few people who had seen and admired Emily Carr's paintings. One of them was Eric Brown, director of the National Gallery in Ottawa. In 1927 he invited Carr to come to Ottawa to exhibit her work and meet other artists. Carr went first to Toronto, where she was anxious to see the work of some Toronto-based artists known as the Group of Seven. She met Lawren Harris, and in his monumental Canadian landscapes she saw the boldness that she was trying to achieve in her West Coast canvases. Harris was equally impressed with Carr's work. Finally, Carr had what she had wanted her whole life: someone to talk to, who understood and respected what she was trying to do.

When she returned to British Columbia, Carr began to paint again. This time, she felt she was creating art as she had always hoped to achieve. First she painted the totem poles; then the mighty trees that had existed before the totem poles; and then the mountains, the beaches, and the sky—the massive forms of nature. Emily gave up the time-consuming boarding house and moved to a small cottage. Finally, in her sixties, she was a successful artist. Her paintings were exhibited in Canada, the United States, and Europe, and were sought after by collectors. For ten years, encouraged by her Group of Seven friends, she was intensely productive.

Then, in 1937, Carr had a heart attack. After that, her health was not good enough to travel to remote native villages. She turned to writing, again with great success. In 1941, when she was seventy years old, she published *Klee Wyck*, about her experiences with West Coast native people. Klee Wyck means "laughing one" in the language of the Nuu-chah-nulth. Not only was this a popular book, it won the Governor General's Award for Literature.

In 1942 Carr's account of her Victoria childhood, *The Book of Small*, was published ("Small" was her childhood nickname). In 1944, *The House of All Sorts*, about the apartment house she ran, appeared. A few months after she died, in 1945, at the age of seventy-three, her autobiography, *Growing Pains*, was published. Today, the Vancouver Art Gallery has a special room devoted to her work, holding almost 200 pieces. In 2000, one of Emily Carr's paintings, *War Canoes*, sold for over $1 million.

# Sam McLaughlin
## 1871–1972

I T ALL STARTED WITH AXE HANDLES. As a boy, Robert
McLaughlin, the son of Irish immigrants who came to
Canada in the 1830s, helped to clear the land so that his pioneering family could start a farm. Cutting down trees, he learned
all about the strength and usefulness of different kinds of wood.
When his family needed extra money, he began to make and sell
axe handles. Soon he branched out into whiffletrees (crossbars
for wagons and ploughs) and other wagon parts. In 1867 he built
his first cutter—a light, horse-drawn sleigh—based on a picture
he had seen in a catalogue. That was the humble beginning of
the McLaughlin Carriage Works in Enniskillen, Ontario.

By the time Sam McLaughlin, Robert's third son, was born in 1871, the McLaughlin Carriage Works had moved to Oshawa. Robert McLaughlin had invented a steering mechanism that made carriages much safer to drive, and business was booming.

From his childhood, Sam McLaughlin loved speed. He had a penny farthing, an early kind of bicycle with the seat perched high above the large front wheel. He often rode his bicycle to Toronto from Oshawa, a distance of nearly 50 kilometres. The road was a toll road; however, Sam McLaughlin, on a bicycle, didn't have to pay the fee charged to horse-drawn carriages.

When McLaughlin finished high school at age sixteen, he went to work as an apprentice upholsterer in his father's factory, earning $3 a week. From this, his father—whom everyone called "the Governor"—deducted $2.50 for room and board. Sam McLaughlin worked from seven in the morning until seven at night. After three years of this, he was fed up. He went to work for a carriage company in New York state, where he was well paid and learned about plant management. He returned home at age twenty-one. The Governor not only welcomed him back, but handed over all the money he had deducted from his son's paycheques. Over the next few years, Sam McLaughlin designed more than 140 different kinds of carriages and sleighs for the family business.

The McLaughlin Carriage Works had taken over several existing factories, originally built for manufacturing furniture, and expanded them when more space was needed. In 1899 a fire destroyed all of it. With the insurance money and a loan from the town of Oshawa, the McLaughlins rebuilt. The new plant was large and so strongly built that it still forms part of the current plant. In 1901, when Sam McLaughlin was thirty, he became a partner in the carriage works with his father and older brother George. By 1905 the company was producing 25,000 carriages and sleighs a year and shipping their vehicles as far away as South America and Australia. The McLaughlins became very wealthy.

Around this time, McLaughlin took his first ride in an automobile, a Ford that belonged to the company bookkeeper, Oliver Hezzlewood. "I think it ran on one cylinder," McLaughlin recalled many years later. "It had no doors, top, or windshield." The bookkeeper asked McLaughlin if he could create something to protect riders from the weather. He came up with a rubberized sheet that fit over the car, with four holes cut out for the driver and each of the passengers to stick their heads through. In return, Hezzlewood invited McLaughlin to drive his car whenever he wanted.

In 1905 people would stop and stare when the strange new contraption they called a "horseless carriage" rattled by. The Ford Motor Company in the United States was only two years old. In all of the city of Toronto, there were fewer than thirty automobiles. Most roads were either dirt or gravel. But to Sam McLaughlin it was clear that cars were the future of transportation. George agreed with him, but it was going to be hard to convince the Governor.

McLaughlin used his summer holidays to visit every American car-maker he could find. One of them was Richard Pierce of Buffalo, whose plant assembled the beautiful Pierce-Arrow automobile by hand, piece by polished piece. They sold for $3,000—roughly $60,000 in today's dollars. But Pierce quietly told him, "Cars like this have no future, Mr. McLaughlin. I would advise you against trying to make them." McLaughlin agreed that he should think about a lower-priced car that could be mass produced. Eventually he made his way to William Durant, who had just bought the Buick Motor Company.

When McLaughlin returned home, he was convinced that the McLaughlin Carriage Works should begin manufacturing

Buicks in Canada. He laid out all his collected research for the Governor, who listened quietly and then said simply, "If you think you can make a go of it, go ahead."

In 1907 the McLaughlin Motor Car Company was launched, producing 193 cars with bodies designed by McLaughlin and engines supplied by the Buick Motor Company of Flint, Michigan. These were the first motor cars actually assembled in Canada. The most popular model was the Model F: a two-cylinder, 22-horsepower touring car with a red chassis and a gleaming wine-coloured body, which cost $1,400.

In the United States, William Durant was buying up automobile companies and establishing the business that became General Motors. It was becoming harder for small, independent automobile manufacturers to compete with American auto giants in the making such as GM and Ford. In 1918 the McLaughlins sold their car company to General Motors. McLaughlin became president of General Motors of Canada, and his brother George became vice-president. By the early 1920s, assembly lines in the Canadian plant were churning out thousands of Buicks, Chevrolets—which sold for less than half the price of the original McLaughlin Buicks—and Oldsmobiles. GM Canada was soon employing 3,000 people.

McLaughlin had married Adelaide Mowbray, a schoolteacher, in 1898. In 1915 the McLaughlins moved into their dream home in Oshawa—a fifty-five-room mansion called Parkwood. The best architects and craftsmen of the day worked on the house, and the couple furnished it with antiques and art from around the world. The house also boasted bowling lanes and an indoor swimming pool. The 12-acre grounds featured an Italian garden and squash courts. Here they raised their five daughters in luxury.

In 1942 McLaughlin retired from day-to-day management of GM Canada, although he remained chairman of the board until

1967, when he was ninety-six. In 1951 he established the McLaughlin Foundation, which supported medical education and research. Among his many other charitable donations were funding for a planetarium in Toronto, an intensive-care unit for the Hospital for Sick Children, also in Toronto, a medical and engineering building for Queen's University, and a library for the University of Guelph. Oshawa received a hospital, a library, and a Boy Scouts camp with an Olympic-sized pool.

Sam McLaughlin was a Companion of the Order of Canada, and received several honorary degrees from Canadian universities. However, his favourite honour had come early in his business career, when he was appointed honorary lieutenant-colonel in the 11th Ontario Regiment. For the rest of his life, he was known to his employees as "Colonel Sam."

Sam McLaughlin died in 1972, four months after his 100th birthday. By then, General Motors of Canada employed 20,000 people and produced 500,000 vehicles a year. The company had come a long way from the little axe-handle business started by a farm boy.

# Nellie McClung

## 1873–1951

FOR NEARLY FORTY YEARS after Confederation, in 1867, women in Canada were not allowed to vote in elections or to run for office. Until 1929 women were not even considered persons under Canadian law. Many people worked very hard to ensure that these inequalities were changed, but few were as important to the cause as Nellie McClung.

Nellie McClung was born Helen Letitia Mooney at the family farmhouse in Grey County, near Owen Sound, Ontario. She was the sixth child born to a strict Scottish-Presbyterian mother and an Irish-Methodist father, and religion would always play an important part in her life. In 1880, when Nellie was only six, the Mooney family moved to Manitoba to find better farmland on the banks of the Souris River. Because the family was so poor, Nellie had to work on the farm from a very young age. She could not even go to school until she was ten years old. Still, she proved to be a bright student. Just before her sixteenth birthday, in 1889, Nellie went to Winnipeg for a five-month teacher-training program at the Winnipeg Normal School (teachers college).

Nellie's first teaching job was in the tiny town of Somerset, Manitoba, about 160 kilometres (100 miles) southwest of Winnipeg. In a one-room schoolhouse, she taught children from grades 1 to 8. On the day she arrived in Somerset, the school trustee met her at the train station and explained that the town would not be able to pay her. Somerset was a farming community, and the district's entire crop had been destroyed by a hail storm. She would at least be able to live rent-free with the trustee's family and she would not have to pay for her own meals.

While she was teaching in Somerset, Nellie also began to write. She filled notebook after notebook with ideas and stories about her impressions of the events of the day. One of her early influences was E. Cora Hind (see her biography), who published articles in the *Winnipeg Free Press*. Another important influence was Annie McClung. They met during Nellie's first year in Somerset, when she began attending church in the nearby town of Manitou. Annie was the wife of the local Methodist minister, and she taught the Young Ladies' Bible Class. After meeting Mrs. McClung, Nellie remarked that "She is the only woman I have ever seen whom I should like to have for a mother-in-law." When Nellie moved to Manitou to teach school there in 1892, she went to live with the McClung family. In 1896 she married Wesley McClung, and Annie did indeed become her mother-in-law.

Encouraged by Annie, Nellie McClung did more and more writing. In 1902 she entered a short-story contest sponsored by an American magazine. The publishers convinced her to expand her story into a novel. *Sowing Seeds in Danny* would be the first of sixteen books she wrote. The book—a tale of Danny and Pearlie Watson and their life on the Prairies—was published in 1908 and sold more than 100,000 copies. McClung made quite a lot of money from the book and, together with Wesley's earnings as a successful pharmacist, she was able to raise her own five children in a much more comfortable home than she had grown up in.

Despite her own happy home life, Nellie McClung was not blind to the poverty and despair of others. Many people blamed these problems on alcohol. The modern concept of drinking responsibly was not a part of life in the 1890s and early 1900s. It was not uncommon for a working man to drink away his entire paycheque in a tavern, then return home, drunk, to beat his wife or children. A man was the master of his home, and there were no laws against such behaviour.

Many women first got involved in politics in an effort to enforce Prohibition (the complete ban on alcohol sales). Through her mother-in-law's influence, Nellie McClung had become involved with the Women's Christian Temperance Union, an anti-alcohol organization. When *Sowing Seeds in Danny* became a success, Annie arranged for Nellie to read from her book at a Temperance Union meeting. From that point on, Nellie McClung became an important speaker on women's issues.

Through her work with the Temperance Union, Nellie McClung came to believe that Prohibition—and other issues that were important to women—would not be taken seriously until women were given the right to vote. The right to vote is known as suffrage, so women who worked towards votes for women became known as suffragettes or suffragists. After Wes and Nellie moved their family to Winnipeg in 1911, McClung became actively involved as a suffragist. She would speak at more than 400 meetings over the next twenty years, often delivering three speeches a day on speaking tours that took her across Canada, the United States, and Great Britain. She was a lively, entertaining speaker who could attract large audiences to listen to her. Still, the job of winning votes for women proved to be difficult.

In McClung's home province of Manitoba, Premier Rodmond Roblin was very much against the idea of giving women the right to vote. In an interview with Nellie, Roblin mockingly told her, "I don't want a hyena in petticoats talking politics at me. I want a nice, gentle creature to bring me my slippers." On January 27, 1914, McClung led a delegation, representing the Temperance Union, the Canadian Women's Press Club, and the Political Equality League, before the Manitoba legislature. Again Premier Roblin dismissed her scornfully, but Nellie McClung would get her revenge.

In the fall of 1914, McClung portrayed the premier in a stage play called *The Parliament of Women*. She mimicked Roblin's voice and gestures perfectly in a performance that made his views look foolish, by using his own arguments against men instead of women. The play was a tremendous success and many newspapers were forced to admit that Roblin's opinions were outdated. McClung and her associates supported the Liberal Party in Manitoba's election of 1914, but still Roblin's Conservatives won. However, a scandal soon afterwards brought his party down.

Liberal leader T.C. Norris had claimed to support women's suffrage, but he changed his mind once he took power in 1915.

He said he would not introduce voting rights for women unless the suffragists could show there was enough support for the idea. McClung and her colleagues collected 40,000 signatures on a petition, and on January 27, 1916, Manitoba became the first province in Canada to pass a bill giving women the right to vote.

Nellie McClung, however, was no longer in Manitoba to enjoy the privilege she had worked so hard for. Wes McClung's business had taken the family to Edmonton in December of 1914. Nellie had continued to push for women's rights in Alberta, and both that province and Saskatchewan changed their voting laws shortly after Manitoba did. Women finally won the right to vote in all federal elections in 1918. During these years, which coincided with the First World War, McClung also supported the Canadian war effort and the Red Cross. Her oldest son, Jack, had become a soldier in 1915 and survived to return home in 1919.

In 1921 Nellie McClung ran as a Liberal candidate in the Alberta provincial election and won. In the legislature, she supported social issues such as medical and dental care for school children, married women's property rights, and mothers' allowances. Though she was defeated in 1926, McClung was soon helping to lead the fight that would see the Canadian government appoint its first woman senator in 1930. To do this, McClung and four other women (Emily Murphy, Henrietta Muir Edwards, Louise McKinney, and Irene Parlby) had to go to court to challenge the ruling that women were not persons under the law. In those days, the highest court of appeal for Canadians was still in England, and this case went all the way to the Privy Council in London. Finally, on October 18, 1929, the decision was announced that women were indeed persons.

McClung remained busy in the later years of her life. She and Wes moved to Victoria after his retirement in 1935, and

Nellie continued to write books. She was also named a governor of the Canadian Broadcasting Corporation (CBC) in 1936 and was selected as a delegate to the League of Nations (forerunner of the United Nations) in 1938. She and Wes celebrated their fiftieth wedding anniversary in 1946. On September 1, 1951, Nellie McClung died at the age of seventy-seven.

# William Lyon Mackenzie King
## 1874–1950

W ILLIAM LYON MACKENZIE KING was short and a bit pudgy. He had few close friends and was never married. He seemed to lack the charisma of other political leaders, and his speeches were often ordinary. Yet Mackenzie King served as prime minister of Canada three times. In all, he was leader of the country for nearly twenty-two years—far longer than any other prime minister. King believed the most important thing for a government to do was prevent problems. His ability to seek the middle ground and keep all parts of Canada united was the key to his political success.

"Willie," as his family called him, was born in the town of Berlin (later renamed Kitchener), Ontario. The second of four children, but the first-born son, Willie was doted on by his mother, Isabel Grace Mackenzie. She had named him after her father, William Lyon Mackenzie, the political radical who had rebelled against the injustice of British rule in Canada in 1837. Ironically, King's grandfather on his father's side had been a British Army officer at the time of the rebellion.

Political discussions were customary in the King household as young Willie grew up, and he was always aware of his mother's wishes that he enter public life as her father had. His parents were devout Presbyterians, and King considered becoming a minister. He earned a law degree from the University of Toronto in 1896, but never became a lawyer. While studying in Toronto, King saw the desperate plight of the city's poor. When he continued his education at the University of Chicago, he spent time working with Jane Addams, who had become famous for her work with that city's poor immigrants. King later studied economics and earned a doctorate at Harvard University. (He is the only Canadian prime minister to have obtained a Ph.D.)

When King returned to Toronto in 1897, he wrote a series of newspaper articles, focusing attention on the terrible living conditions of the city's working poor. The stories attracted the attention of William Mulock, a friend of King's father and a cabinet minister in Sir Wilfrid Laurier's new government. Mulock asked King to prepare a more detailed study, and many of the recommendations in the report he wrote for Mulock became Canadian policy. In 1900 Mulock told King that the government wanted him to become the editor of the new *Labour Gazette*. King had also been offered a teaching position at Harvard, but he decided to accept the publication job. Later that year, the government created a department of labour, Mulock was placed in charge, and King became his deputy minister. He was only twenty-five years old, but the course of his life had now been set.

Mackenzie King, as he now signed his name, travelled around the country, helping to settle strikes, using an even-handed approach. The experience he gained helped the government introduce the Industrial Disputes Investigation Act in 1907. This legislation would help guide Canadian labour relations for the rest of the century. King also learned about how the process of governing worked. He saw that change only came slowly and that great care had to be taken.

Sir Wilfrid Laurier had long been aware of King's good work. He planned to expand the department of labour and suggested that King could become its minister if he ran for office in the general election of 1908. King was elected in Waterloo North, a riding that included his hometown. His parents were watching proudly from the House of Commons gallery when Laurier introduced King as a new member of his cabinet in 1909. Though King continued his good work as minister of labour, the country was growing tired of the Liberal Party, which had formed the government since 1896. After issues like the Naval Debate and Reciprocity (free trade with the United States) further damaged Laurier's popularity, the Conservatives won the next election, in 1911. (For more information about these topics, see the biographies of Robert Borden and Wilfrid Laurier.) William Lyon Mackenzie King lost his seat and, after just two years in the cabinet, he was out of a job.

For the next three years, King supported himself by writing for newspapers, making speeches, and doing organizational work for the Liberal Party. In 1914 he was hired by the Rockefeller Foundation in the United States. He directed the company's department of industrial relations and helped restore labour relations after a strike in the Colorado minefields. This is a controversial period in King's career, since the strike had been long and bloody and was ruthlessly put down by mine owners. However, the experience resulted in his writing *Industry and Humanity*, which was published in 1918. In this book, King outlined his belief that governments should take more responsibility for the health and well-being of citizens.

The year 1917 was difficult for King: his beloved mother passed away and he lost another election. The general election that year was fought over the issue of Conscription (compulsory military service). The First World War had been raging since 1914, and the Conservative Party had decided that Canada must do more than just send volunteers to help England win the war against Germany. The issue of Conscription bitterly divided the country. Most English-speaking Canadians supported the idea, but most French Canadians were bitterly opposed. The issue also divided the Liberal Party, with most prominent English-speaking members leaving Laurier to join Robert Borden's new Union government.

For Mackenzie King, the election of 1917 proved to be a turning point. Because he had not abandoned Sir Wilfrid Laurier, he was seen as the best choice as the next leader of the Liberal Party. Indeed, after Laurier died in 1919, King was selected at the leadership convention. By now, the Conservative/Union government (under Borden and then Meighen) was running into problems: Quebec blamed the new leader, Arthur Meighen, for his prominent role in the Conscription crisis, and Western Canada was angered by the party's poor record on labour issues, such as the 1919 Winnipeg General Strike. (For more about this strike, see the biographies of J.S. Woodsworth and Robert Boyd Russell.) When the next election was held, in 1921, the Liberals returned to power. William Lyon Mackenzie King was now prime minister of Canada.

King was steady but unspectacular during his first term in office. He made small reductions in the tariff rates (taxes on foreign goods) to try to increase trade, and he balanced the government's budget for the first time since 1913. He also began to assert more Canadian independence from England. Confident in the job he had done, Mackenzie King called another election in 1925. But he was in for a surprise. The Conservatives took 116 seats, while the Progressives (a new party representing Western farmers) took 24. The Liberals won just 99. King himself was defeated in his York North riding, though he was later re-elected in a by-election in Saskatchewan.

Despite the fact that the Conservatives held more seats, King believed he could gain the support of the Progressive Party and remain in power. However, by June of 1926, a scandal in the customs department threatened to bring down his government. King asked Governor General Julian Byng to dissolve Parliament and call a new election. Ordinarily, a governor general did what the prime minister told him, but this time Byng refused. King resigned as prime minister and Conservative leader Arthur Meighen formed a new government. Soon afterward, Meighen lost his hold on the House of Commons and this time there had to be another election. Mackenzie King made sure that Byng's behaviour was the only important issue, asking the country if a British official should have the right to refuse a Canadian prime minister. Voters forgot about the customs scandal and the Liberals won the election.

Now heading a majority government, King began to put in place some social reforms. He introduced old-age pensions in 1927. He also supported unemployment insurance, but was unable to convince provincial governments to agree with him.

When the Great Depression began in 1929, unemployment became a major problem as the economic slump put people out of work all over the world. Governments fell everywhere, and King's Liberals were no exception. They were defeated in the election of 1930.

As it turned out, the Liberals were fortunate to be in opposition. The Depression was much worse than anyone had anticipated, and could not have been stopped no matter what policies R.B. Bennett's Conservative government tried. By the next election, in 1935, Canadians were desperate for a change. Campaigning on the slogan of "King or Chaos," the Liberals were voted back into power. William Lyon Mackenzie King was prime minister for the third time.

King did little more than Bennett had tried to do to ease the Depression, though he did promote more trade with the United States, to improve unemployment, and he negotiated a new trade deal with Britain. But soon the threat of another war in Europe would overshadow all other concerns. Though Canada was gaining more and more independence, it was still part of the British Empire. If Britain went to war, Canada would have to play its part. However, Mackenzie King was determined that he would not let any issue divide the country as it had been divided during the First World War.

The German army invaded Poland on September 1, 1939. England and France declared war two days later. On September 10, 1939, Canada also declared war on the Nazis. Mackenzie King's initial policy was that there would be no Conscription; instead, Canada would provide a volunteer army and all possible economic aid. King called an election for March of 1940. With the Canadian economy finally returning to normal, people were not anxious for a full-fledged war effort. The idea of Conscription had little appeal, and the Liberals scored the biggest election victory to that point in Canadian history. The Party won 181 seats to 40 for the Conservatives and 8 for the Co-operative Commonwealth Federation (forerunner of the NDP). Public opinion was soon to change, however.

By June of 1940, Hitler's armies had defeated France, and it seemed possible that Britain might lose the war. Canada would have to do more to help. Workers in Canadian industries were working in shifts around the clock to produce trucks, planes, and other supplies for the war effort, but it was plain that more soldiers would have to be sent. In 1941 Conscription was introduced for home defence only. This was a policy that Quebec could support. Then in 1942, a national vote was held to ask if people would release the government from its promise of no Conscription for the war in Europe. The majority of Quebeckers voted no, but in the rest of Canada, the majority voted yes. Still, King tried to hold off. As he put it, the solution was "Not necessarily Conscription, but Conscription if necessary." But by 1944, he was forced into action, sending to Europe the Canadian soldiers who had originally been conscripted for home defence. Of the 15,000 conscripts who were sent overseas late in the war, only 2,463 ever saw action.

The war was costly for Canada: by the time it finally ended in 1945, more than a million Canadians had enlisted, and some 42,000 had been killed. However, Canada had emerged more united than before, and the economy was stronger than ever. During the war years, King's government had finally been able to establish unemployment insurance and also create a Family Allowance Act, to improve the condition and nutrition of young children. In June of 1945, Mackenzie King led the Liberals to another election victory. He retired as prime minister on November 15, 1948, and left Parliament for good in April of 1949. He died on July 22, 1950.

Throughout his life, William Lyon Mackenzie King kept a detailed diary. After his death, Canadians learned some strange things about their longest-serving prime minister. Although he was devoutly Christian, he believed in spiritualism and the occult. In fact, he believed that he could communicate with his mother through seances and the use of mediums, which included his dog, Pat.

# Lucy Maud Montgomery

## 1874–1942

IN 1904, Lucy Maud Montgomery wrote in her notebook of story ideas, "Elderly couple apply to orphan asylum for a boy. By mistake a girl is sent them." A year later, Montgomery had finished a book-length manuscript based on this idea. Over the next several years, she sent it off to five different publishers—but all of them rejected it. It took until 1908 for *Anne of Green Gables* to find a publisher. As soon as the book appeared, however, it became a best-seller, reprinted six times in its first five months. Lucy Maud Montgomery had succeeded in her dearest wish—to become a writer. Today, red-haired Anne Shirley, the brave and cheerful orphan who finds happiness, is known and loved by millions of readers around the world.

Lucy Maud Montgomery was born in Clifton, Prince Edward Island, in 1874. Her mother died when she was not quite two. Maud's father turned her over to the care of his wife's parents, and he left for Saskatchewan. Maud's stern grandparents lived on a farm near the small settlement of Cavendish, not far from the northern coast of the island. The farm was surrounded by apple orchards, but there were few visitors, so Maud spent much of her early childhood alone. However, her vivid imagination and her love of nature's beauty kept her from feeling lonely.

When she was nine, Maud began to keep a diary and write poems. Already she had dreams of one day being a published author. Many years later, she explained, "To write has always been my central purpose around which every effort and hope and ambition of my life has grouped itself."

By 1890 Maud's father had settled in Prince Albert, Saskatchewan, and had remarried. He sent for his sixteen-year-old daughter to join him, and her grandfather took her out West on a long, exciting journey by boat, train, and stagecoach. Prince Albert was a bustling new community, but Maud was more attracted to its natural setting: a river valley surrounded by forests, lakes, and bluffs. While she was in Prince Albert, she had her first work published: a thirty-nine-verse poem about a Prince Edward Island legend. However, her happiness didn't last. She missed Cavendish, and did not get along well with her new, young stepmother. In 1891 her father brought her back to Prince Edward Island.

After high school, Lucy Maud Montgomery studied English literature at Dalhousie College in Halifax. While she was still a student, she began to sell her short stories and poems to Canadian and American magazines. Then she became a teacher to support herself, but she continued to pursue her dream of a writing career. On dark winter mornings, before her school day began, Montgomery would wrap herself in a heavy overcoat against the cold—and write. Around this time, she fell passionately in love with a young PEI farmer, but she decided she could not marry him because he was uneducated and not her social equal.

In 1898 Montgomery's grandfather died and she returned to the farm to help her grandmother. She lived on the Cavendish farm for the next thirteen years, except for a brief time when she worked as a proofreader—checking spelling and punctuation—for a Halifax newspaper. She continued to write, often stories with fantastic plots that her editors asked for. "I don't much care for writing such," she admitted about one of these stories, "but they offer a good price for it. It deals with a lost ruby, a lunatic . . . a mysterious turret chamber."

In 1901 Montgomery wrote proudly to a friend that she could now make a living by her pen. In 1902 she earned $500 from her stories and poems—equal today to about $10,000. Finally, in 1908, came the huge success of *Anne of Green Gables*. Her first royalty cheque (money paid to her for each book sold) was for $1,790—worth more than $30,000 today—and this was followed by many more large cheques for years to come. "The dream dreamed years ago at that old brown desk in school has come true at last, after years of toil and struggle," Montgomery wrote.

Montgomery became a celebrity. She was invited to Boston by her publisher, and met with all the famous literary people of that city. Mark Twain wrote her a fan letter. When the governor general of Canada came to visit Prince Edward Island, he requested a meeting with the author of *Anne*. The public—and her publisher—demanded a sequel. Montgomery responded with three more books about Anne, and each one was a great success.

In 1911 Montgomery's grandmother died, and Montgomery was finally free to marry her long-time fiancé, the Reverend Ewan Macdonald. She did not love him, but she respected him and believed that they could have a good life together. They moved to Ontario, where Macdonald was to become the minister at the Leaskdale Presbyterian Church. Montgomery never lived in Prince Edward Island again.

During the busy Leaskdale years, Montgomery had two sons (a third son was born dead). A minister's wife had many responsibilities, including organizing church events and comforting troubled members of the congregation. In addition, Montgomery had a heavier burden. Her husband suffered mood swings and periods of black depression (then known as melancholia). The disease was not understood, and there was no effective treatment. Montgomery was determined that her husband's congregation would never know about it, because then he might lose his job. As she struggled to keep her husband's illness a secret, she sometimes became sick with worry herself, but she always put on a cheerful face for the community.

Through all of this, Montgomery continued to write—four more books about Anne, as well as the *Emily* trilogy. Emily's life was based closely on her own. All but one of the books she wrote in Ontario were set in Prince Edward Island. In all, Montgomery produced twenty-two books of fiction, as well as almost 500 poems and as many short stories. In addition, she kept a huge diary, which was published many years after her death.

Through all of her adult life, Montgomery missed Prince Edward Island and looked forward to visiting. However, living in Leaskdale had one advantage. She was able to visit Toronto, where she could meet other authors and attend plays. She was a sought-after speaker for women's groups and schools. As her fame grew, Montgomery was honoured in various ways. She was the first Canadian woman to become a fellow of Britain's Royal Society of Arts and Letters, and she was named an Officer of the British Empire.

In 1926 the Macdonalds moved to Norval, Ontario, and in 1935, when Ewan retired, they moved to Toronto. Lucy Maud Montgomery died in 1942 at the age of sixty-eight, outlived by her husband by just one year. She was buried in her beloved Cavendish.

Today, Montgomery's fame is greater than ever. The stories of Anne and Emily have been adapted for stage, film, and television. Anne even appeared on a Canadian postage stamp in 1975. The books have been translated into more than fifteen languages, and are especially loved in Japan, where Montgomery's most famous heroine is known as *Akage no An*—"red-haired Anne." Tourists from all over the world flood into Prince Edward Island every summer to see the places around Cavendish that Lucy Maud Montgomery loved.

# Tom Thomson

## 1877–1917

ON JULY 16, 1917, the body of a man was discovered floating in Canoe Lake in Algonquin Park. His feet were wound with copper fishing line and there was a bruise on his forehead. The body was soon identified as Tom Thomson, who had last been seen on July 8, setting out to go fishing. Officially, his death was listed as an accidental drowning, but several writers who have studied the case believe that he was murdered. The death of Tom Thomson has become one of Canada's enduring mysteries. Books have been written about it; in addition, novels and a feature film have been based on fictionalized versions of Thomson's romantic life and puzzling death. But what is certain is that his death deprived Canada of one of its most remarkable artists at the height of his genius.

Thomas John Thomson was raised on the family farm in Leith, near Owen Sound, Ontario. He was the sixth of ten children, and his large and happy family was full of musical and artistic talent. Almost all the children played musical instruments; Tom could play the cornet and the violin, but his favourite instrument was the mandolin. His father liked to sketch, and Tom began to draw at an early age. As a child he entertained his brothers and sisters by drawing caricatures and having them guess who they represented.

Young Tom loved the out-of-doors and thought he might become a naturalist when he grew up. But his grades were poor, partly because he was often kept out of school by a lung ailment. He never went to high school; in fact, he did not finish grade school.

In 1899 Canadian troops were heading to the Boer War in South Africa to support Britain in its war against the Dutch settlers (Boers). Thomson tried to enlist but was turned down for medical reasons. He then became an apprentice machinist at a foundry in Owen Sound. However, he could not get along with his boss and he quit after a few months, returning to the family farm in time to help with the harvest.

Finally Thomson settled down and attended business college, which he completed when he was twenty-four. His brother George had gone to Seattle, Washington, and started his own business college. In 1901 Thomson joined him there. He designed a poster, a newspaper advertisement, and a business card for George's school. Using these as samples of his proficient work in design and lettering, he was able to get other commercial art assignments in Seattle. He and George had a fine time in Seattle, spending the evenings at plays or concerts, or making music with their friends.

In 1904 Thomson proposed marriage to a woman named Alice Lambert. The young woman was startled by the proposal, even though she was very fond of Thomson, and she giggled nervously. Thomson felt so humiliated by her reaction that he turned his back on her, returned to his boarding house, packed his suitcase, and left Seattle at once. She never saw him again.

Thomson moved to Toronto and got a job at a photo-engraving company as a commercial artist. On the weekends he visited his parents in Owen Sound or sketched outdoors, with crayons and watercolours, near the Humber River. For the first time, he began to take art seriously and took night classes at the Ontario College of Art. Then, around 1907, he went to work for Grip Limited, another commercial design company. This was the turning point in Thomson's life.

At Grip Limited, he had a group of co-workers who would later become famous Canadian artists, including Arthur Lismer, Frederick Varley, Franklin Carmichael, and J.E.H. MacDonald. These men had more art training than Thomson, but they were impressed by his natural artistic ability and helped him with his painting technique. Because Thomson had no place to paint, he was allowed to use the Grip building on weekends.

In the spring of 1912, Thomson first boarded a train for the Canoe Lake Station in Algonquin Park. Later that summer he travelled along the Spanish River to the Mississagi Forest Reserve, west of Sudbury. He was now, for the first time in his life, using oil paints to sketch from nature. Encouraged by his fellow artists at Grip Limited, Thomson turned one of his sketches from that summer into a painting. Called A Northern Lake, it was purchased by the Government of Ontario for $250. Inspired by Thomson, some of the other artists began to make excursions to Northern Ontario to paint. After they saw Thomson's sketches, Lismer later recalled, "We realized that the Northland was a painter's country."

The group of artists who worked at Grip Limited shared a common goal. All of them believed that they should try to capture, on canvas, the unique grandeur of Canada's wilderness, and that the best way to do this was to paint outdoors, directly from nature. By 1913 they had formed bonds with several other like-minded artists. Lawren Harris, an artist from a wealthy family, helped finance the Studio Building in Toronto, where artists could both work and live. The artists invited A.Y. Jackson from Montreal to come and paint with them there. Jackson and Thomson became particularly close, sharing studio space in 1914 and influencing each other's work. Around this time, too, Thomson met Dr. James MacCallum, who had promoted MacDonald's work and now became Thomson's patron. With financial help from MacCallum, Thomson left his job and began to paint full-time.

In 1914, when the First World War broke out, Thomson volunteered, as he had in the Boer War, but was turned down again—his feet were deemed unfit for marching. Thomson thought this was ridiculous, since he regularly hiked 30 kilometres in the Ontario wilderness. While A.Y. Jackson and Frederick Varley went overseas, Thomson's life fell into a satisfying and productive pattern.

Thomson went to Algonquin Park every summer and was never happier than when paddling his canoe on lonely northern lakes. He became an expert canoeist and was renowned for his skill as a fisherman. At times he worked as a fire ranger or guide in the park, to make a little extra money. But he tried to sketch every day—quick, vivid sketches with oil paint on small wood panels. The details were not as important as capturing the colours and the patterns of light and shadow. He would give most of these small sketches away to friends or sell them for $5 or $10. Today they are greatly admired for their bold brush strokes and intense colour. Many art critics prefer them to his finished canvases.

Every winter Thomson moved into a renovated construction shack behind the Studio Building and made paintings based on some of his sketches. In the winter of 1916–17, he produced his most famous painting, *The Jack Pine*, now in the collection of the National Gallery of Canada.

Thomson was buried at Canoe Lake, but later his family moved him to the family plot in Leith, Ontario. His friends could not believe that an experienced outdoorsman could get his fishing line entangled around his feet and tip out of his canoe. There was talk of a heated argument with another fisherman the night before his death. Now that so many years have gone by, it is likely the mystery may never be solved.

Thomson only began painting seriously in 1913 and five years later he was dead. In those years, however, he produced some 500 panel sketches and 40 canvases. His talent did not emerge until he became part of a group of artists who encouraged him. But, at the same time, they had come to see him as *their* inspiration. "Without Tom the North Country seems a desolation of bush and rock," A.Y. Jackson wrote. "My debt to him is almost that of a new world." Three years after Thomson's death, Harris, MacDonald, Lismer, Varley, Carmichael, Jackson, and Frank Johnston held a joint exhibition for the first time as the Group of Seven.

# Arthur Currie
## 1875–1933

THE GERMANS OCCUPIED VIMY RIDGE in September of 1914, barely one month after the First World War had begun. Vimy Ridge is a long, whale-shaped hill rising 60 metres above the Arras region of France. The hill gave the Germans a commanding view of the Allied forces, which made it very difficult to attack. As many as 50,000 French soldiers had died trying to take Vimy Ridge back from the Germans in 1915. Nearly as many British troops were killed or wounded in the area in 1916, and the Germans had come to believe that Vimy Ridge was impregnable. Canadian Major-General Arthur Currie felt otherwise: "If the lessons of war have been thoroughly mastered;

if the artillery preparation and support is good; if our intelligence is properly appreciated, there is no position that cannot be wrested from the enemy by disciplined, well-trained and well-led troops attacking on a sound plan."

The Canadians who attacked Vimy Ridge on April 9, 1917, were commanded by British General Julian Byng, with Currie as Byng's chief Canadian lieutenant. The two men insisted that the attack on Vimy Ridge must be well planned and well rehearsed. Every soldier had to know where he was going and what landmarks to aim for. Until this point in the war, British soldiers had attacked in large waves. Currie suggested the use of small platoons. British tradition called for soldiers to be organized by function, but Currie wanted each Canadian platoon to include riflemen, machine gunners, and bombers.

The victory at Vimy Ridge was a turning point in the First World War and helped establish the reputation of Canadian soldiers as the best fighters on the Western Front. Many historians have pointed to the victory at Vimy Ridge as the beginning of Canadian independence from British rule. Though Arthur Currie had helped to devise their strategy and had led his Canadian First Division to victory in their own part of the battle, he wanted the credit for the success at Vimy Ridge to be given to his soldiers. "Each and every man knew just exactly where he was going in the attack, and what he was going to do when he got there."

Unlike most British generals in the First World War, Arthur Currie did not have an army background, nor did he come from a military family. He was raised on a farm in the town of Strathroy, not far from London, Ontario. He was the third of seven children born to William and Jane Curry. (Arthur would later use the Scottish spelling of his last name to reflect the family's Scottish roots.)

Young Art, as he was known as a boy, attended a one-room schoolhouse in the nearby town of Napperton. He did well enough in his studies to qualify for entrance to the Strathroy Collegiate Institute in 1888 at the age of twelve. (One of the student teachers at the school during Art's first year was Stephen Leacock.) Art developed into an excellent student at Strathroy Collegiate. He also sprouted to his full adult height of six feet, four inches and weighed close to 200 pounds while still a teenager.

Art showed a keen interest in debate while in school and hoped to use his impressive skills by becoming a lawyer. However, his father's unexpected death in October of 1891 put an end to those plans. Older brother John would take over operation of the family farm, but there was no longer enough money to send Art to university. He would study to become a teacher instead, graduating in the spring of 1893. However, times were tough, and he was unable to find a job.

In May 1894, Arthur Currie decided to leave home for Victoria, British Columbia. He finally found a teaching job there, in the autumn of 1895. He also found the woman he was going to marry: Lucy Sophia Chaworth-Musters, who was known simply as Lily. They were wed on August 14, 1901. A short time before the wedding, Currie had given up teaching for a better-paying job in a Victoria insurance company. Later, he would be involved in real estate.

Less than three months after his marriage to Lily, Arthur Currie became a captain in his British Columbia militia unit. He had joined the 5th Regiment of the Canadian Garrison Artillery back in 1897 and had risen rapidly through the ranks. Had he not suffered from a serious stomach ailment in the fall of 1899, he certainly would have offered his services to the Canadian volunteer army that was raised to help England fight in the Boer

War. However, even without active service, Currie continued to receive promotions. In 1906 he was made a major and was named second-in-command of the entire 5th Regiment. By 1909 he was a lieutenant-colonel and commander of the regiment. Between 1910 and 1913, Currie commanded the 5th to numerous awards for marksmanship and general efficiency.

In 1913 Arthur Currie left the 5th Regiment for the challenge of creating a brand-new militia unit. The 50th Regiment would be affiliated with one of the most famous units in the British Army: the Gordon Highlanders. Currie officially took command on January 2, 1914, just eight months before the outbreak of the First World War. Sam Hughes, Canada's minister of militia and defence, had met Currie before, and his son Garnet was a major in the 50th Regiment. This connection helped Currie earn command of one of the four infantry brigades being raised for service in the Canadian Army at the newly built military camp in Valcartier, Quebec. Currie arrived in Valcartier on September 1 and was soon placed in charge of the Second Canadian Infantry Brigade. He had gone from leading a few hundred men to commanding 4,000 soldiers. He worked extremely hard at Valcartier, impressing not only Sam Hughes but also Canadian Prime Minister Robert Borden.

The first contingent of the Canadian Expeditionary Force set sail for England on October 3, 1914. The soldiers were to complete their training at Salisbury Plain before they joined the battle. When the war had broken out in August, many people predicted it would be over by Christmas. It wasn't, and on February 12, 1915, Currie and the Second Brigade were sent to fight in France.

Currie's Second Brigade had seen very little action until they arrived in the Belgian town of Ypres on April 14, 1915. Eight days later, the Germans attacked French colonial troops with poison gas. Many of the French troops turned and ran. Those who tried to stay and fight were choked to death by the gas. When the clouds dispersed, the Germans had a clear path to the Canadian line. The Canadians, backed by British reinforcements, were able to hold off the Germans for two days. Then, on April 24, 1915, the Germans attacked the Canadian soldiers with poison gas. The Canadians tied handkerchiefs soaked with their own urine—which gave some protection from the gas—over their noses and mouths and managed to hold their ground.

On September 14, 1915, Arthur Currie was promoted to major general. Still a few months away from his fortieth birthday, he was one of the youngest men to achieve this rank during the First World War. He was also named commander of the Canadian First Division. Currie commanded his troops throughout the bloody Somme offensive of 1916, in which there were over 24,000 Canadian casualties. One year later, he was knighted by King George V after the victory at Vimy Ridge. Then, in June of 1917, Currie succeeded Julian Byng as commander of the entire Canadian Corps. He was also promoted to lieutenant-general.

As corps commander, Sir Arthur Currie was better able to put the skill and initiative of Canadian troops to use. In the fall of 1918, the corps achieved an unparalleled run of military successes that became known as "Canada's 100 Days." These victories helped to finally bring the war to an end, but Currie was concerned that the Canadian soldiers were not receiving enough credit for their efforts. Perhaps for that reason, Canadian troops continued to fight right up until the moment the armistice went into effect at 11 a.m. on November 11, 1918. In the final minutes of the war, Canadian troops were able to liberate the Belgian town of Mons, which the British army had lost to Germany in the very first days of the fighting, back in 1914.

Currie's relationship with Sam Hughes had worsened during the course of the war. Later in his life, Hughes and others would attack Currie over the events at Mons. Rumours claimed that as many as eighty Canadian soldiers had been killed in the last hours of the war, although the actual number was six. In 1928 Currie went to court to sue a politician who spread lies about Mons in a newspaper article. Soldiers came from across Canada to testify on Currie's behalf. He won the case, but received only $500 in damages.

After the war, Sir Arthur Currie served as inspector-general of the Canadian militia and became the first general in the Canadian Army. In 1920 he accepted the position of principal and vice-chancellor of McGill University in Montreal. He retained that post until his death in 1933.

# John McCrae
## 1872–1918

O N MAY 3, 1915, John McCrae sat on the back of a parked ambulance and gazed sadly at the military cemetery nearby. Among its simple wooden crosses, blood-red wild poppies swayed in the breeze. He took out his notebook and began to write: "In Flanders Fields, the poppies blow, between the crosses, row on row. . . ." McCrae's poem became the most famous poem of the First World War, and because of his poem, the poppy became the symbol of death in battle. Every year on Remembrance Day, Canadians wear poppy pins to honour those who died in all our country's wars.

John McCrae was not a soldier at the time he wrote the poem. He was a doctor serving in a field hospital in Flanders (an area of Belgium) during a bloody battle at Ypres. He was forty-two years old—old enough to be the father of the young soldiers he was treating. Before the war and the tragic events that inspired his poem, he had accomplished many other things.

McCrae was born and raised in Guelph, Ontario, the second son of a lieutenant colonel. However, the McCrae family owed its prosperity to a woollen mill, established in Guelph by McCrae's Scottish immigrant grandfather. The two McCrae boys were brought up to be patriotic and proud of Canada's connection to the British Empire. While John McCrae was in high school, he joined the Highland Cadet Corps and later joined the local militia—an artillery regiment commanded by his father.

McCrae also loved literature and poetry, an interest he shared with his mother, and he had a deep affection for animals. For a long time, he could not decide whether he wanted to be a doctor or a veterinarian. When he was sixteen, McCrae won a scholarship to the University of Toronto. While he studied biology and then medicine, he wrote poems and short stories, which were published in various magazines. For his own enjoyment, he also made pen-and-ink sketches.

McCrae had to take a year off from his studies because he had severe asthma, which would trouble him throughout his life. During that year, he taught English and mathematics at the Ontario Agricultural College in Guelph. In 1894, he graduated from the University of Toronto's faculty of medicine at the top of his class. He interned first at Toronto General Hospital and then in Baltimore, at Johns Hopkins, where he trained under the guidance of Sir William Osler, a world-renowned physician.

All this time, McCrae had kept up his ties with the military. While he was at university, he joined a Toronto militia, the Queen's Own Rifles, and rose to the rank of captain. When war broke out between Britain and the Dutch settlers (Boers) in South Africa, McCrae postponed taking up a fellowship he had been offered at McGill University in Montreal. He set off by ship in December 1899 as an officer in the Royal Canadian Artillery. He came under fire several times during his year in South Africa, but more upsetting to him were the dirty and disorganized military hospitals—and the suffering they caused wounded soldiers. After the Boer War, McCrae was fully committed to being a doctor, and he resigned from service in the artillery regiment.

The years between 1902 and 1914 were productive and fulfilling for McCrae. He was a highly respected physician, with appointments at Montreal General Hospital and Royal Victoria Hospital. In 1909 he became a lecturer at the McGill Medical School and, with his older brother, also a doctor, wrote chapters for a medical text edited by Dr. William Osler. McCrae wrote more than forty medical papers, on subjects ranging from Montreal slum conditions to tropical diseases.

The unmarried McCrae had a busy social life as well. He dined out often with friends, and he belonged to the Pen and Pencil Club, a club for literary men whose members included Stephen Leacock. McCrae was still writing and publishing poetry, and he was also an outdoorsman who enjoyed camping, hiking, and mountain climbing. In 1910 McCrae accompanied the governor general of Canada, Lord Grey, on a canoeing expedition that retraced a Hudson's Bay Company fur-trade route from Lake Winnipeg to Hudson Bay.

When Canada went to war against Germany in 1914, McCrae signed up at once and was appointed a brigade surgeon with the rank of major. Unlike younger men who had never been to war, he had some sense of what was ahead, and was not eager to go overseas. But he wrote that, as a single man, he felt it was his duty to go, and his conscience wouldn't let him rest if he stayed in Canada.

Life was miserable at the front line. Shelling and the movement of armies had turned the landscape into a sea of mud. Neither side in the war could gain much ground. Instead, they dug in, living for months on end in filthy trenches. Occasionally, they went "over the top"—out of the trench to face shells and machine-gun fire that maimed and killed—to gain a few kilometres, sometimes only a few metres, of territory. And then the wounded and dying would stream into the field hospital where McCrae was stationed, and he would work around the clock trying to ease pain and save lives.

He kept up his spirits by writing daily letters home to his mother and other family members. He had brought his horse, Bonfire, with him from Canada, and he sometimes wrote whimsical letters to his young nephews and nieces that were supposed to come from Bonfire, and were even "signed" with a hoofprint.

By the spring of 1915, McCrae had seen a great deal of death and suffering, but one death particularly affected him. On May 2, a close friend and former student of his, Alexis Helmer, had been killed by a shell burst. Since no chaplain was available, McCrae performed the funeral ceremony. The next morning, he scribbled "In Flanders Fields" into a notebook during a twenty-minute break. McCrae showed it to some of his friends, and someone—possibly McCrae, possibly a fellow officer—sent the poem to the British magazine *Punch,* which published it in December. Within a few months, the poem had been reprinted around the world.

By the time the poem appeared in print, McCrae had been transferred to a hospital in Boulogne, France. He worked long hours in the makeshift hospital, which was set up in the ruins of a college. It was cold and damp and McCrae's asthma returned. He had a wracking cough that he could not shake; finally, a lung infection forced him to go into a hospital for military officers. As soon as he felt strong enough, he returned to his medical duties. He wrote in one of his letters, "The cruel cold is still holding. Everyone is suffering and the men in the wards in bed cannot keep warm. . . . For my own part I do not think I have ever been more uncomfortable. To go to bed is a nightmare and to get up a worse one."

On January 4, 1918, McCrae developed pneumonia. This time he was too worn down to fight off illness. Two days later, he developed meningitis and died on January 28. He was buried with military honours in Wimereux Cemetery in France, not far from the fields of Flanders. In his funeral procession was Bonfire, riderless and bearing McCrae's boots backward in the stirrups—a military tradition to symbolize a fallen soldier.

# Billy Bishop

## 1894–1956

O N THE MORNING he was to meet King George V
of England, Billy Bishop was late arriving at
Buckingham Palace. In the general confusion over
which medal he was to receive (he was, in fact, to receive three
medals that day), the King was kept waiting even longer. Finally,
when it came time for him to march into the room where the
King awaited, the heel on one of his boots squeaked loudly.
Bishop was embarrassed, but the King was not bothered. With a
dignified air, he pinned the medals of the Military Cross, the
Distinguished Service Order, and the Victoria Cross—England's
highest medal of bravery—onto the uniform of the young

Canadian. It was the first time the King had presented all three medals to one living man. These awards were an amazing accomplishment for a boy whose school days at the Royal Military College had been noted only for hijinks—and low marks.

Billy Bishop was born and raised in Owen Sound, Ontario. His father was a lawyer, and his older brother, Worth, was an excellent student, but Billy never did well in school. He preferred outdoor activities like hunting and riding. When he was fifteen, Billy read about the first airplane to be built in Canada and was determined to build one of his own. He tried to fly it off the third-storey roof of his family home, but it crashed to the ground. Amazingly, he was unhurt.

At the age of seventeen, Billy decided to follow in the footsteps of his brother, Worth, who had recorded the highest marks in the history of Kingston's Royal Military College. His parents hoped the school's discipline would help improve his studies, but it did not. In his third year at RMC, in 1914, he was nearly expelled after stealing a canoe to try to sneak into town and meet some girls. Next, he was caught cheating on his exams. He felt sure that he would be kicked out of school when the new term began. Since war had broken out during summer vacation, Billy Bishop decided to join the army.

When the First World War began, very few people were aware of the horrors in store, and most thought the fighting would be over quickly. Bishop enlisted in September and was assigned to the Mississauga Horse, a Toronto cavalry unit. He was later transferred to the 7th Canadian Mounted Rifles, another cavalry unit.

Though Billy Bishop had gone to war on horseback—one of the oldest methods of fighting—he would soon be involved with the world's most modern weapon: the airplane. The loathesome mixture of mud and manure during his training in England convinced him to change. In his autobiography, *Winged Warfare,* Bishop wrote that "I had succeeded in getting myself mired to the knees when suddenly from somewhere out of the storm, appeared a trim little airplane. . . . When I turned to slog my way back through the mud my mind was made up. I knew there was only one place to be on such a day—up above the clouds and in the sunshine . . . I was going to meet the enemy in the air."

The fastest way into Britain's Royal Flying Corps was not as a pilot but as an observer. It turned out that Bishop had tremendously good eyesight and by January 1916 he was sent to France in this new role. He became excellent at spotting enemy formations, using the camera, and directing bombs. Still, he wanted to become a pilot, but it took some good luck to make that happen. While in London during the spring of 1916, he met an influential woman who had known his father in Canada. Lady St. Helier was able to arrange for Bishop to go to air-training school.

Though his keen eyesight and uncanny accuracy with a machine gun would make Billy Bishop the most famous Canadian flying ace of the First World War, he was never one of the best pilots when it came to actually flying a plane. For example, on March 24, 1917, he crash-landed his plane in front of a general and was very nearly sent back to training school. Major Jack Scott convinced the general to let Bishop fly again, and the next day he shot down his first German plane. He would be allowed to remain with 60 Squadron.

At this time, the life expectancy of a fighter pilot in the Royal Flying Corps was just three weeks. But Billy Bishop beat the odds. On April 7 and 8, 1917, he forced two German observation balloons out of the sky, helping to clear the way for the Canadian troops who attacked Vimy Ridge on April 9.

By the end of May, he had shot down more than twenty planes and would soon launch the strike that won him the Victoria Cross.

Bishop and Albert Ball, the leading British flying ace, had considered attacking a German airfield together. When Ball was killed, Bishop decided to go it alone. In the early morning hours of June 2, 1917, he ambushed seven planes that were just getting ready to take off. Four of them managed to get into the air, but Bishop shot them all down. Because no one witnessed his attack, some would later doubt Bishop's word, but much evidence has been found to back his claim.

Soon after his airfield attack and his meeting with the King, Billy Bishop was sent back to Canada. With the war becoming less popular at home, it was hoped the great hero could convince more people to volunteer. While at home, he also married his fiancée, Margaret Burden, the granddaughter of Timothy Eaton. He returned to France to head up the new 85 Squadron in May 1918, but was soon removed from active duty. He had become so famous and admired that it was feared the loss of morale would be too great if he were killed. On his last day in the air on June 19, Bishop shot down five planes, bringing his total to seventy-five. Only Germany's Manfred von Richthofen, the "Red Baron," had shot down more. (Sometimes Bishop's total is listed as seventy-two, but this does not include the three balloons he brought down.)

After the war ended, Billy Bishop opened an airplane passenger service with fellow Canadian Victoria Cross pilot William Barker. Unfortunately, the company failed after less than two years. Later, Bishop would become a successful businessman. In 1938 he was made an honourary air marshall in the Royal Canadian Air Force. When the Second World War broke out in 1939, he did much to help the RCAF with recruitment and training. His book *Winged Peace* was published in 1944, and his views helped the United Nations form the International Civil Aviation Organization in 1947.

Billy Bishop passed away in his sleep in Palm Beach, Florida, in 1956. He is buried in the family plot in Owen Sound. His childhood home there is now a museum.

# J.S. Woodsworth
## 1874–1942

HE TRAVELLED THE COUNTRY by train, refusing comfortable sleeping cars for the ordinary, afford-able day coach. Even as a frail old man with snowy white hair and beard, he insisted on carrying his own bags. For meals, he would eat sandwiches that he brought with him and make a cup of tea in the kitchen provided for those who could not afford the dining car. When he reached his destination, he would usually stay in the home of a supporter. It was not that he couldn't afford better service, it was simply that he had more important things to spend his money on.

As a young man, J.S. Woodsworth had every opportunity to accept a life of leisure. Trained as a Methodist minister, like his father, he could have settled down in a prosperous parish, spreading the word of God the way people were used to hearing it. Instead, he chose to use his beliefs to champion the cause of the country's underprivileged.

James Shaver Woodsworth was born on a farm just outside of Toronto. When he was very young, his father worked in Northern Ontario, serving as a travelling minister in far-flung communities. In 1882, when J.S. was eight years old, the family moved to Manitoba. A few years later, James Woodsworth, Sr. was appointed superintendent of Methodist Missions in the North-West (a region that stretched from the Manitoba/Ontario border all the way to British Columbia). As the eldest son, J.S. would often accompany his father on his trips across the West. After he graduated from Wesley College at the University of Manitoba in 1896, it was not surprising that he decided to follow in his father's footsteps. J.S. Woodsworth gained his degree in theology from Victoria College (University of Toronto) in 1899. While studying there, he met Lucy Staples, the woman who would become his wife.

It was also while he was in Toronto that Woodsworth learned of the larger issues facing the Methodist Church at the dawn of the twentieth century. Among the most important was the concept of social gospel. Traditional Christian beliefs preached personal salvation and prepared people for a "better life" in heaven. However, those who favoured the social gospel believed it was the duty of all people to concern themselves with the brotherhood of mankind and work towards love and equality on earth. A visit to England helped Woodsworth make up his mind to dedicate himself to these ideals.

Woodsworth travelled to London to continue his education at Oxford University in the fall of 1899. He spent several weeks at Mansfield House in the slums of London's East End, where university people offered various services to the city's poor. Woodsworth helped to prepare meals, and the images of small children "watching me pour out the soup, pleading for just a little more of the thicker soup near the bottom," stayed with him always.

After returning to Canada in 1900 and marrying Lucy in 1904, J.S. Woodsworth became the assistant pastor at Grace Church in Winnipeg. At this time, Winnipeg was the gateway between the farms of the Prairies and the industries of the East. As a result, it was one of the most prosperous cities in Canada. People were getting rich from the railways, which helped the city grow, and from the increasing value of the real estate. Banks, brokerage houses, and all sorts of other businesses were booming. But as the rich got richer, the poor seemed to have less and less. Woodsworth spoke out on the evils of greed and the plight of the poor, but the prosperous parishioners of the Grace Church did not want to listen. He left the church in the summer of 1906.

In 1907 Woodsworth became the superintendent of the All Peoples' Mission. This Methodist Mission served Winnipeg's North End, where the city's working class and new immigrants lived. Woodsworth spent six years there, where workers taught English to the immigrants and helped them try and fit into Canadian ways. Woodsworth tried to convince people in the prosperous parts of Winnipeg to help those in the North End, but even if he could collect money for the poor, he knew this was not enough.

Woodsworth became convinced that the best way to help was to "bring about changes in our whole social system that will enable men and women to live out their highest lives." While he was working at the All Peoples' Mission, Woodsworth wrote two books about the plight of Winnipeg's immigrant poor. *Strangers at Our Gates* and *My Neighbour* earned him recognition as one of Canada's leading experts on social issues.

The outbreak of the First World War in 1914 soon saw J.S. Woodsworth speaking out again on an unpopular topic. Woodsworth was a pacifist, which meant he was against all wars. He accepted that individuals might decide for themselves that they wanted to join the army, but he was firmly against Conscription—forcing people to fight. He argued against Conscription in a Winnipeg newspaper, which resulted in his being fired from his government job with the Bureau of Social Research.

Unable to find any work at all in Winnipeg, Woodsworth took a job with a church near Vancouver, but his socialist beliefs soon caused him to be fired from that job, too. Needing to support his wife and a family that had grown to five children, Woodsworth took a job loading and unloading ships in Vancouver. Soon he was involved with the city's labour unions. He also wrote newspaper articles for British Columbia's Federated Labour Party—and his work in Vancouver earned him an invitation to speak out on labour issues back in Winnipeg.

J.S. Woodsworth arrived back in Winnipeg on June 8, 1919. At that time, the city was in the midst of a General Strike—30,000 workers had left their jobs to support better working conditions and recognition for their unions. (For more about the strike, see the biography of Robert Boyd Russell.) The city was virtually shut down, although the strike leaders made sure that essential services—such as bread and milk deliveries—were maintained. Still, the city government in Winnipeg, the provincial government in Manitoba, and the federal government in Ottawa were all against the strikers.

Though people were concerned that the strikers might turn violent, it was attacks against the strikers by soldiers and policemen that eventually brought the strike to an end on June 25. Many of the strike leaders were arrested, as was Woodsworth, who had spoken out on their behalf. The charges against him were eventually dropped, but the events of the Winnipeg General Strike convinced Woodsworth that labourers needed to have a voice in the Canadian Parliament. His belief that better working conditions could be established by working with the government made him a socialist, as opposed to communists (who wanted to change the entire system).

In the spring of 1921, Woodsworth joined the Independent Labour Party. That December he was elected to Parliament as the member for Winnipeg Centre. Woodsworth was the first man ever to be voted into the Canadian House of Commons from an organized socialist party. The Liberal Party won the election of 1921, but Canadian politics was changing. Since Confederation, there had only been two parties: Liberals and Conservatives. Suddenly, there were new parties popping up, to represent farmers and the working class. Woodsworth was able to use the changes to his advantage, because Liberal Prime Minister William Lyon Mackenzie King needed the support of the new parties to stay ahead of the Conservatives. It would take years of badgering to get the Liberal Party to introduce unemployment insurance, but Woodsworth was able to persuade King to create old-age pensions in 1927.

Once in Parliament, J.S. Woodsworth travelled the country, tirelessly trying to educate the public about the values of social democracy. Still, many of the social issues Woodsworth championed were being ignored—even after the Great Depression of the 1930s began to put many people out of work. So, in 1932, Woodsworth began to put together all the small political groups that supported his beliefs. The result was the creation, in 1933, of Canada's third official political party—the Co-operative Commonwealth Federation, or CCF. (It would later change its name to the New Democratic Party, or the NDP.)

As the leader of the CCF, J.S. Woodsworth not only worked to establish social reforms, he also spoke out against racism. Anti-Asian prejudice was at its height during an election in British Columbia in 1937. Citizens of Asian descent were not allowed to vote in that province, and it was illegal for them to work in many professions. Woodsworth insisted that this must change. His strong beliefs may have cost some CCF candidates the election that year, but eventually the laws would change.

By the end of the 1930s, the world was on the brink of another war. Officially, the CCF believed in Woodsworth's pacifist views, but when the time came to vote on Canada's participation in the war effort, only one man rose in the House of Commons to speak out against it—J.S. Woodsworth. Once again, Woodsworth stood up for what he believed in, even though he knew it was the unpopular view. This time it cost him the leadership of the party he had created. Eight months later, he suffered a stroke. Still, in the election of 1940, he was voted into the House of Commons for the sixth time. This time, however, the lifelong fighter was in no condition for a final battle. Unable to take part in the House of Commons in 1941, he left Ottawa for his family home in Vancouver. He died there on March 21, 1942.

# Robert Boyd Russell
## 1888–1964

I N 1911 a young immigrant named Robert Boyd Russell stepped off the train in Winnipeg. He had been born into a working-class family in the industrial city of Glasgow, Scotland. At the age of twelve, Russell had been forced to leave school to earn a living, becoming an apprentice machinist in a Glasgow factory. He was angered by the injustices he saw in a society where most people had to work long hours for little pay, while a privileged few lived in luxury. He thought that in the young and growing Canadian West, conditions might be better for the working man. He made up his mind to emigrate with his friend Bert Hampton and Bert's sister, Peggy, whom Russell married soon after they arrived in Canada.

As an experienced machinist, Bob Russell easily found work at the Canadian Pacific Railway's Weston Shops in Winnipeg. Here, thousands of workers repaired and maintained engines, built railway cars, and even manufactured rails for the CPR. However, he quickly realized that, once again, he was in a city where there was a huge gap between rich and poor. Railway executives, bankers, and other wealthy people lived in mansions in the South End of Winnipeg. Workers like Russell, many of them recent immigrants, were crowded into the slums of the city's North End. Soot from the Canadian Pacific railyards floated over the neighbourhood, blackening walls and windows. There were few parks where children could play and few city services— drains and sewers were poor and garbage was seldom collected.

Russell's father had been a trade-union organizer in Glasgow. Russell, too, believed that the only way for workers to win better wages, shorter working hours, and safer working conditions was through trade unions. Individual workers could too easily be fired if they stood up for themselves; but as members of a union, workers could bargain collectively (as a unified group), which gave them a much stronger position. If management refused to negotiate with them, they could withhold their labour; that is, they could go on strike. Russell became a union organizer for the International Association of Machinists (IAM), encouraging his fellow workers to band together to fight for better working conditions.

In the early years of the twentieth century, most unions—like the IAM—were craft unions, which represented only a particular type of skilled labour. Employers could pit one union against another by, for example, saying that if the carpenters got higher pay, there would be less money available for the bricklayers.

Russell believed that workers would be able to bargain more effectively if they belonged to industrial unions, which would include every worker in a particular industry, whether they were skilled or unskilled. In fact, he took the idea one step further. Inspired by an American organization called the Industrial Workers of the World (known as "the Wobblies"), Russell began to advocate for a union that would bring together *all* workers. The name he favoured for this organization was the One Big Union, or the OBU.

During the First World War, from 1914 to 1918, Russell continued his union work. He spoke out against the way wages were controlled during the war, even though employees in war-related industries were asked to work harder and harder, in unsafe conditions. Many other Canadian unionists accepted the constraints the government asked for during the war, feeling that it was their patriotic duty, but not Russell. It seemed clear to him that only the rich and powerful had anything to gain from the war. However, ordinary people were the ones who were asked to make sacrifices, either on the battlefield or at home.

In March 1919, Russell attended a gathering of top labour leaders in Calgary. Over 200 delegates attended, and they drafted a number of resolutions. They called for a five-day workweek. They called for the end of the capitalist system, which seemed to them to enrich a few at the expense of the many. They supported Russell's ideas for the One Big Union. If workers' demands were not met in a particular work setting, then all workers could go out on strike to support them. This is known as a general strike.

All levels of government and owners of businesses, especially in the West, watched gatherings like this with growing nervousness. While Russell and other unionists felt that they were working towards a better and more just world, to government and business, their call for the complete transformation of society made them dangerous men. Less than two years earlier, the Czar of Russia had been overthrown in a violent Communist revolution. Many were worried that militant union leaders might be planning a revolution in Canada.

In the spring of 1919, Russell's union—the IAM—and other metal trades banded together in the Metal Trades Council, with Russell as secretary. The metal workers presented their demands to three ironworks companies: recognition of their right to bargain collectively, an eight-hour day, and overtime pay for extra hours. When the companies refused to bargain with them, 12,000 metal workers walked off the job on May 15. To show their support, over 20,000 workers in other industries, both unionized and non-unionized, also walked off the job. The strikers included garbage collectors, delivery men, firefighters, telephone operators, and mail carriers. The 200-member police force voted to go on strike, but the Central Strike Committee, which included Russell, asked them to stay on the job to keep order.

During the six weeks of the Winnipeg General Strike, the ordinary life of the city came to a halt. The spring of 1919 was particularly hot in Winnipeg, and within a few days, the air was full of the stench of uncollected garbage. There was no telephone or telegraph service. There were no newspapers. Restaurants and theatres were closed. Milk and bread were not delivered. The city government could no longer function, since workers refused to obey its orders. So it was up to the Strike Committee to make sure that basic services were provided. They gave permission to delivery people to make deliveries of bread and milk. Their vans had large signs on the side: "Permitted by Authority of the Strike Committee." This was meant as a reassuring gesture, but it had the opposite effect. Many people took it as a sign that revolutionaries had now taken over the city.

To deal with the strike, the business people of Winnipeg formed the Citizens' Committee of 1000. This committee accused the strikers of being Bolsheviks—Communists—who supported the violent overthrow of the government. Over the next few weeks, the city fired most of its police force, who were sympathetic to the strikers, and replaced them with 2,000 "Specials"—civilians wearing white armbands and armed with wooden batons.

The strikers had vowed to keep their gatherings peaceful, and at first they were. But as the long, hot weeks went by with no settlement of the strike, tempers began to fray. The workers vowed to march publicly every day until their demands were met. City officials countered by calling for the Royal North-West Mounted Police to keep order. The anti-striker Specials were aggressive, and had no experience in crowd control. They waded into a group of strikers who were listening to speeches on June 10, and fighting broke out.

At 2:00 a.m. on June 17, authorities arrested Bob Russell and seven other strike leaders. They were charged with conspiracy to overthrow the government. (In November, Russell would be sentenced to a two-year term in the Stony Mountain federal penitentiary—the harshest sentence given to any of the strike leaders. However, he was released after less than a year.)

The striking workers were outraged by the arrests. Although there was now a ban on demonstrations, they staged a parade on Saturday, June 21. Demonstrators smashed windows and overturned a streetcar. Then the Royal North-West Mounted Police rode into the crowd, firing three volleys that killed two men and injured several others. The frightened crowd tried to disperse, but about 200 people became trapped in an alleyway. The Specials attacked them with batons and gunfire from both ends of the alley and at least thirty more people were injured. Within five days the strike was over. The workers had failed to win any major concessions, but shocked by the violence of "Bloody Saturday" and without their leaders, they had no energy to continue.

The Winnipeg General Strike looks very different to us now from the way it did in 1919, when so many people feared that it was the beginning of a revolution. Most historians now agree that the majority of strikers simply wanted a living wage and the right to collective bargaining.

It would take three more decades before collective bargaining rights would become established in Canadian law. But leaders of the strike had an impact on Canadian policy making long before that. In 1920, four of the arrested strike leaders were elected to the Manitoba legislature, three of them while still serving prison terms. The following year J.S. Woodsworth, who had supported the strikers and had been arrested, was elected as an Independent MP. (See Woodsworth's biography for more about this.)

When he was released from jail, Bob Russell continued to work as an organizer for the OBU. At its peak, in 1920, the union had nearly 50,000 members across Canada. The craft-union movement opposed it, however, as did many employers. The OBU was further weakened when its leaders disagreed among themselves about their policies. In 1921 Russell ran for Parliament, backed by the Socialist Party and the OBU, but he was defeated by the Communist candidate, Jacob Penner.

By 1923 the OBU had only about 5,000 members. Russell soldiered on as its general secretary, negotiating better wages, organizing pension funds, and setting up a summer camp for workers' children. In 1956 the last remaining members of the OBU joined the newly organized Canadian Labour Congress. Russell continued as executive secretary of the Winnipeg District Council of the CLC until ill health forced him to resign in 1962.

Bob Russell had been a labour leader, devoted to improving conditions for working people, for over fifty years. In September 1964 he rode in the place of honour at the head of Winnipeg's annual Labour Day parade, but he was now so ill that he knew this would likely be his last parade. Later that day, he had some unusual visitors at his home: a delegation from the Manitoba government brought him an "Address of Appreciation" signed by the premier and the labour minister of the province. A man who had once been accused of trying to overthrow the government was finally being honoured for his work as a Canadian labour leader and for his "many and notable contributions to the general welfare of the city." Just a few days later, Russell died at the age of seventy-six.

# Angus Walters
## 1882–1969

THE ORIGINAL *BLUENOSE* SCHOONER was built low
to the water, and her three tall masts seemed to stretch to
the sky. Her sleek wooden hull was painted a shiny
blue-black, making her many white sails look all the more
dazzling. There was no doubt she was beautiful, but what was it
that made her so fast? Some said it was because the boat was just
a bit longer at the waterline than most. Others believed that her
timbers had been toughened by a particularly hard frost. Still
others credited the almost magical relationship between the ship
and her captain; he could almost speak to her, according to the
old-timers of Lunenburg, Nova Scotia.

The *Bluenose* schooner was the culmination of nearly 150 years of shipbuilding excellence in the Canadian Maritime provinces. Sadly, at the time the *Bluenose* was built in 1921, she already represented the end of an era. Iron-hulled ships powered by steam had all but replaced wooden sailing boats. Still, the schooner would give Nova Scotians, and Canadians everywhere, a sense of pride and joy as she won race after race. In 1937 the great ship was commemorated with an engraving on the back of Canada's dime. The image of the *Bluenose* at full sail can still be seen there. The man behind the ship's success was Captain Angus Walters. Like the *Bluenose* herself, he was part of a long tradition of Canadian maritimers—that of the courageous fisherman.

Angus Walters of Lunenburg, Nova Scotia, was one of twelve children born to a sea captain and his wife. He first went to sea in 1895 at the age of thirteen, working on his father's ship as a "throater"—the person who cuts the heads off fish after they're caught. By fifteen, he was a doryman, fishing from the small craft (known as a dory) that is launched from the main ship.

Walters became the captain of his own vessel while still a teenager. Since the 1780s, the fishermen of Nova Scotia had engaged in a friendly rivalry with American fishermen from the coastal towns of Maine and Massachusetts. They competed to see not only who could catch the most fish, but also to see which boats would be first to reach the fishing grounds of the Grand Banks. More importantly, the ships also raced to be the first back into the harbour at Lunenburg or Gloucester (in Massachusetts). The first ship back would control the market and set the price. Young Angus Walters quickly earned a reputation both as an excellent fisherman and as a sailor who could get the most speed out of his vessel. He was a quiet and unassuming man on shore, but at sea he was a tough master.

Angus Walters was thirty-eight years old in 1920 when the owner of the Halifax *Herald* decided to turn the friendly rivalry between Nova Scotians and New Englanders into a formal race. Since 1851, the America's Cup had pitted sailors from around the world against one another, but they raced in yachts designed especially for competition. The International Fisherman's Trophy series would be for real fishing boats—and it would offer a cash prize of $4,000 (an amount equivalent to almost $35,000 today). In September of 1920, Angus Walters raced his boat, the *Muriel B.*, against another Lunenburg ship, to see who would represent Canada against the American fishermen. Unfortunately, he raced his boat so hard that it broke its mast. As if that weren't bad enough, the ship that beat Walters was then outraced by the American boat from Gloucester.

Determined to win the race the following year, Nova Scotians commissioned the building of a new schooner. The ship was designed by William Roue and would be captained by Angus Walters. At a time when most sailing ships were named after women (usually the wife or daughter of the captain or the owner), this ship would be known by the same colourful moniker that was affectionately given to all Nova Scotians. It would be called the *Bluenose*.

After spending the spring and summer of 1921 fishing off the Grand Banks, Walters captained the *Bluenose* to victory over all other Nova Scotian competitors in October. He then defeated the *Elsie* of Gloucester in two straight races (in a best-of-three series) to win the Fisherman's Trophy. Now it was the Americans who felt they had to build a special new boat. Their *Henry Ford* defeated the *Bluenose* in a light wind to win the first race in 1922, but with a stiffer breeze blowing in the next two races, Walters captained his ship to victory. The success of the *Bluenose* made Walters a hero across Canada.

In 1923 the *Bluenose* defeated yet another new American vessel, the *Columbia*. However, after a dispute over the rules, Walters returned to Lunenburg without the Fisherman's Trophy. It would be eight more years before the race was held again. In the meantime, the *Bluenose* continued to work as a fishing boat. In 1926 the most famous boat in Canada was nearly sunk in a violent storm that claimed the lives of fifty Lunenburg fishermen. With a fierce wind blowing up waves as high as 14 metres (45 feet), Captain Walters ordered the rest of the crew below deck. He lashed himself to the ship's wheel to keep from being washed overboard. Then he steered the boat through the storm alone, for more than six hours. Rain and snow were pounding down so hard, Walters often couldn't see the waves. "You could hear them coming," he recalled later, "and sometimes I was all under [the water]. I'd just come up [in time] to get my breath."

The *Bluenose* did not race again until 1930, when rules were changed to allow the Canadian schooner to compete in the formerly all-American Lipton Cup race. A group from Boston had paid for the *Gertrude L. Thebaud*, built specifically to beat the *Bluenose*. It did just that, though Walters refused to believe the *Thebaud* was a better boat. "She didn't beat the *Bluenose*," he said. "She beat me. I didn't use my head." Walters and the *Bluenose* got their revenge one year later, when the International Fisherman's Trophy series was revived. The *Bluenose* swept two straight races from the *Thebaud*, winning the first by 3 miles and the second by 2 (about 5 and 3 kilometres respectively).

In the summer of 1933, Angus Walters and his crew sailed the the *Bluenose* up the St. Lawrence River, through Lake Ontario and into Lake Michigan. There, she docked in Chicago to represent Canada at the World's Fair. In 1935, the *Bluenose* sailed to England to take part in the celebrations marking the twenty-fifth year of the reign of King George V. On the return trip across the Atlantic Ocean, the *Bluenose* once again encountered a storm that almost sank her. In fact, the schooner was said to have floated on its side for a full five minutes before finally righting itself. The remarkable recovery added even more glory to the *Bluenose* legend.

Major repairs were required when the *Bluenose* finally limped back into Lunenburg, and a diesel engine was added so that she could keep up with more modern fishing boats. But even with the new engine, it was tough to make a go of things as a fisherman during the Great Depression of the 1930s. When Boston backers offered an $8,000 prize to revive the International Fisherman's Trophy series in 1938, Walters agreed to race one last time. His boat was now seventeen years old and would have to drag its diesel engine, which could not be used in a race. Once again, the *Bluenose* faced the *Thebaud*, this time in a best-of-five series. Each boat won two of the first four races, setting up a dramatic final meeting. Facing a strong wind and rough seas, the *Bluenose* lost one of her sails during the race, but Captain Walters was able to coax his beloved schooner across the finish line first.

Unfortunately, Angus Walters did not receive the promised prize money for winning the Fisherman's Trophy. Eventually, he was paid $5,000, but the *Bluenose* still owed $7,200 for the diesel engine and other repairs. There were suggestions that the Canadian government should take over ownership of the famed schooner, but nothing ever came of it. Finally, Walters scraped together the money himself. He hoped to turn the *Bluenose* into a floating museum, but without government assistance he was forced to sell the ship in 1942. "I knew it was goodbye," said Angus Walters. "We'd seen a lot together in fair weather and foul, and the *Bluenose* was like a part of me."

The most famous ship in Canadian history was used to haul cargo across the Caribbean until it sank off the coast of Haiti in

1946. But the legend of the ship lived on. In the early 1960s, the Smith & Rhuland Shipyard, which had built the original *Bluenose*, began to construct the *Bluenose II*. Built to exactly the same specifications, the new ship was launched in 1963. An eighty-one-year-old Angus Walters was at the wheel. Six years later the Captain passed away, but the *Bluenose II* is still afloat in her home port of Lunenburg, Nova Scotia.

# Lester and Frank Patrick

## (Lester 1883–1960, Frank 1885–1960)

L ESTER PATRICK WAS NINETEEN YEARS OLD when he rode the train from Calgary back to his family home in Montreal in November 1903. After a year of working in the office of his father's lumber business, Lester had gone looking for adventure in Calgary. He had hoped to become a cowboy on a cattle ranch—but he'd never ridden a horse. Instead, he took a dreary job surveying land for the Canadian Pacific Railway. When his employment ended because of cold weather in late fall, Lester decided it was time to go home. But as it turned out, he would not reach Montreal until spring—when the hockey season was over.

Lester Patrick was born in Drummondville, Quebec (halfway between Quebec City and Montreal), and his brother Frank was born in Ottawa two years later. Their father, Joseph, owned a lumber company in a small town near Quebec City, and by 1893 the business was doing so well that he opened an office in Montreal, and moved his family there. It was in Montreal that Frank and Lester Patrick discovered hockey. They hacked sticks out of tree branches and skated on the frozen St. Lawrence River. When the new Montreal Arena was built in 1898, Lester got to practise there with his high-school team. He was becoming one of the best young hockey players in the city, and Frank was not far behind. Lester also played hockey when he got to McGill University in 1901, and he seemed to pay more attention to athletics than to his studies. Soon his father took him out of school and put him to work in the family business. A year later, Lester left for Calgary.

On his way back to Montreal, Lester decided to get off the train in Brandon, Manitoba. He had not played hockey in almost two years, but he wanted to visit three Montreal friends who were playing with the Brandon team. While he was there, he was offered a job as a defenceman. These were the days of seven-man hockey: in addition to forwards, defencemen, and goalies, there was also a position called rover. Defencemen were supposed to help protect their goalie at all times. Forwards were supposed to try to score goals. The rover was expected to help out at both ends of the ice. Lester had played rover in Montreal, and he was used to skating wherever he wanted. One day in a game against Winnipeg, he left his defensive position to rush the entire length of the ice and score a goal. It was the first of many times that a Patrick would make his mark on hockey history.

After he finally returned home, Lester joined the Montreal Wanderers and helped them win the Stanley Cup in 1906 and

1907. At the same time, Frank was becoming a hockey star at McGill University in Montreal. However, when their father opened a new lumber company in the mountains of British Columbia, the two brothers joined the rest of their family out West. But they would not be out of the game for long.

In the winter of 1909–10, a new hockey league was formed: the National Hockey Association. The NHA spent a lot of money trying to attract the best talent. At a time when top hockey players were lucky to earn $1,800 for a season, the NHA team in the tiny town of Renfrew, Ontario, offered Lester Patrick a contract for $3,000. Frank was given $2,000. After Cyclone Taylor signed for $5,250, people called the team the Renfrew "Millionaires."

When the NHA imposed a salary cap for the 1910–11 season, Frank and Lester Patrick decided to stay at home in British Columbia, but once again the hockey world had not heard the last of them. When their father sold his lumber company for $500,000, the Patrick family fortune was invested in building Canada's first artificial ice rinks in Vancouver and Victoria. Then the brothers launched a league of their own—the Pacific Coast Hockey Association.

The PCHA began with three teams in British Columbia: one in Vancouver, one in Victoria, and one in New Westminster. Lester was the owner of the Victoria team. He was also the star player, the coach, and the general manager. Frank was the owner-player, general manager, and coach of the team in Vancouver. He would also serve as the league's president.

The National Hockey Association became the NHL in 1917, but it was Frank and Lester Patrick's Pacific Coast Hockey Association that truly modernized the game. Frank proposed the blue lines, which divide the ice into zones. Lester decided that goalies should be allowed to stop the puck in any way they could, and not be required to stay standing up as the old rules stated. Forward passing was also against the rules in hockey until the Patricks allowed it in the PCHA. They also introduced penalty shots, and assists for players who set up a goal. Before the PCHA, the team that finished in first place during the regular season had always been declared the champion. The Patricks invented the playoffs. The PCHA was also the first Canadian sports league to include American teams, with franchises in Portland and Seattle.

In 1915 Frank's Vancouver Millionaires became the first PCHA team to win the Stanley Cup. In 1917 the Seattle Metropolitans became the first American-based team to win it. Lester's Victoria Cougars were champions in 1925. By then, though, hockey in the West was in trouble. Cities in the East had many more people, and with the NHL now expanding into the United States, there would be even more money to run Eastern teams. Realizing their league could no longer compete, Frank arranged to sell the players to the NHL in 1926, for which the Patricks got about $250,000. The NHL used most of the players on new teams in New York, Detroit, and Chicago.

After the sale, Frank stayed in Vancouver. He invested, without success, in gold mines and oil wells and also organized a new minor hockey league. Lester went to New York to become coach and general manager of the Rangers. His smooth style and good looks helped to make hockey a popular sport in the United States' biggest city. It didn't hurt that in 1927–28, just their second season, the Rangers won the Stanley Cup.

During the 1928 Stanley Cup finals, Lester became a hockey legend. He was forty-four years old and had hardly played during the previous six seasons. However, when Rangers goalie Lorne Chabot was injured in game two, Lester donned the pads himself. (Teams did not carry spare goaltenders back then.) Lester led New York to a 2–1 victory in overtime.

Lester coached the Rangers to another Stanley Cup victory in 1933. Later that year, Frank left Vancouver to become managing director of the NHL. In 1934–35, he became coach of the Boston Bruins. That same season, Lester's son Lynn joined the New York Rangers. Lester continued to coach the team until the 1938–39 season, when his second son Murray (known as "Muzz") also joined him. Both Patrick children became Stanley Cup champions with New York in 1940. Lester was just the general manager that season. Two weeks after the Rangers victory, Frank Patrick returned to the NHL as the business manager of the Montreal Canadiens. He signed several players who would help the Canadiens win the Stanley Cup in 1944, but by that time Frank was back in Vancouver and in semi-retirement.

Lester remained with the Rangers until 1947. That same year, he was elected to the Hockey Hall of Fame. Frank was honoured in 1958. Lester's son Lynn was inducted in 1980, and his grandson Craig Patrick became a Hall of Famer in 2001. Lester and Frank's father, Joseph, whose money supported the PCHA, was named to the British Columbia Sports Hall of Fame in the category of Pioneer in 1998.

When Lester passed away in June 1960, sports columnist Jim Coleman wrote this testament: "Lester Patrick didn't invent hockey but no other man has ever exerted such a lengthy and generally beneficial influence on any sport." When Frank died a mere four weeks later, another columnist claimed, "The modern rule book is a monument to his invention: it still contains twenty-two of the rules he wrote."

It is with good reason that the Patricks are often called "Hockey's Royal Family."

# Tom Longboat
## 1887–1949

I N THE SUMMER OF 1896, the first modern Olympic Games
were held in Athens, Greece, where the ancient Olympics
had been held nearly 3,000 years before. The final event of
the 1896 Olympics was a race to commemorate Pheidippides, the
man who had run 26 miles (in 490 B.C.) to announce the Greek
victory over Persia at the city of Marathon. The Olympic
"marathon" was a huge success, and soon marathon running
became the most popular sport in the world. Crowds of up to
100,000 people would line the streets to watch outdoor races,
while indoor events filled arenas to the rafters. Canadian runners
like James Caffery and Billy Sherring were among the best in

the world, but soon they would be surpassed by the greatest Canadian distance runner of them all—Tom Longboat.

Tom Longboat was the most famous athlete of his day. But he had to battle not only competitors on the racetrack, but also racism. In fact, prejudice against native people was a part of everyday life in Longboat's time. White people didn't even know when they were being insulting. Early in his career, reporters wrote that Longboat's hair looked as if it had been cut with a tomahawk. Even when he became a star, newspapers would call him "The Injun" or "The Redskin." Often, his successes were credited to the white men who trained him, instead of to his own talent and drive.

His family was Onondaga, and Tom Longboat was born in Ohsweken on the Six Nations Reserve, near Brantford, Ontario. His family had to work very hard to maintain its small farm. They had no horse, so even the most strenuous jobs—like plowing and harvesting—had to be done by hand. Tom's father died when Tom was five years old, and though the young boy was soon attending school, he often had to stay home to help his mother on the farm. Still, he would run off from time to time to play lacrosse or go fishing. When he was twelve, Tom began classes at the Mohawk Institute, an Anglican mission boarding school in Brantford. Though the school turned out many important graduates (such as poet Pauline Johnson), Tom hated the time he spent there. He left the school after less than one year, and spent the next few years working as a farm labourer.

While attending the many agricultural fairs held in south-western Ontario farm country, Tom Longboat discovered competitive running. He met Bill Davis, a Mohawk from Ohsweken, who had finished second behind James Caffery at the prestigious Boston Marathon in 1901. Davis filled Tom's head with stories of racing. On Victoria Day in 1905, Longboat decided to enter the five-mile race at nearby Caledonia. He finished second.

After training himself, using a regimen of jogging and long-distance walking, Tom Longboat won the Caledonia race as an eighteen-year-old in 1906. At the urging of Bill Davis, he continued to train while spending the summer working on a farm. Then, in the fall of 1906, he entered the annual "Around the Bay" race in Hamilton, Ontario. The 20-mile (32-km) event attracted all of the top runners in Canada. It was an amateur competition, which meant no cash prizes, but there was plenty of betting. Odds on the unknown Tom Longboat winning the race ranged between 60–1 and 500–1. He wore a loose-fitting jersey, bathing-suit bottoms, and cheap canvas running shoes. Fans laughed at his awkward style: he kept his hands down low, near his waist, while most others pumped their elbows high. The race favourite was John Marsh, and he set a fast pace. Fans watched in surprise as Longboat stayed with him, step for step. Then, with about 8 kilometres to go, Longboat exploded past Marsh. In the end, Tom won the race by three minutes, finishing in a time of 1:49:25.

A mere ten days after his win in Hamilton, Longboat entered the 15-mile (24-km) Ward Marathon in Toronto. This time he beat prominent Toronto runner Bill Cummings by three minutes. Cummings had a second chance back in Hamilton at a 10-mile (16-km) race on Christmas Day. The two runners matched each other step for step over the first 14 kilometres, until Longboat finally pulled away. His time of 54:50 knocked two minutes off the previous course record.

Tom Longboat moved to Toronto and began formal training at the city's West End YMCA. He had been virtually unknown a year earlier, but now, when he entered the famous Boston

Marathon in April of 1907, he was favoured to win it. Not only did he live up to expectations, but his time of 2:24:24 broke James Caffery's record by a full five minutes. When Longboat returned to Toronto after the race, the whole city celebrated his victory. Thousands of fans lined the street as marching bands led Longboat from Union Station to City Hall in a torchlight parade. Throughout 1907 he continued to win a series of shorter races, and he set himself up as the favourite to win the marathon at the 1908 Olympics in London, England.

During the summer of 1907, Longboat had left the YMCA to train with Tom Flanagan at the Irish Canadian Athletic Club. Flanagan's flamboyant management style raised some doubts as to whether Longboat was actually still an amateur athlete (only non-professionals could compete at the Olympics), which could cause some trouble at the London Olympics. When Longboat collapsed during the Olympic marathon after running nineteen miles in gruelling heat, many people were suspicious. Some even accused Flanagan of drugging the great runner in order to win bets he had placed against him. Nothing was ever proven, and Flanagan would continue to manage Longboat for almost two years.

Longboat considered retiring after the Olympic disappointment, but Flanagan urged him to continue. Soon, Longboat joined the professional circuit, and took part in a series of races that would prove he was the best in the world. On December 15, 1908, Longboat beat Dorando Pietri of Italy in a professional race at Madison Square Garden in New York. Three weeks later, Longboat outran Pietri again. Then, on February 5, 1909, he beat England's Alfie Shrubb to win the professional championship of the world.

In the days leading up to the race with Shrubb, there had been concerns about Longboat's condition. He wanted to rest after two gruelling races, but Flanagan wanted him to keep training. Angry over their disagreements, Flanagan sold Longboat's contract to another manager. Longboat was outraged, but many people sided with Flanagan, labelling Longboat "lazy." Still, acting as his own manager, he had an excellent racing season in 1912. But the marathon craze was nearing its end, and he retired as a runner in 1913. The First World War began in 1914, and in 1916, Longboat joined the Canadian Army.

Much of Tom Longboat's military career was spent winning races for army sports teams. However, he also saw action in France as a dispatch runner, carrying messages, much as Pheidippides had done in ancient Greece. Longboat was wounded twice, and was once even declared dead. In fact, when he returned to Canada after the war, he found that his wife had married someone else because she thought she was a widow. Soon afterwards, Tom married a woman from the Six Nations Reserve and began raising a family.

During his best three years as a professional runner, Tom Longboat had earned $17,000. Even after all of his expenses were paid, this was a considerable sum of money. (At that time, the average worker might earn $30 per month.) He had been very generous with his income, buying a new home for his mother and other presents for family and friends. Much of his money, though, had been lost on bad business investments. By 1919 he was just another Canadian soldier who was looking for a job, now that the war was over.

Longboat found work briefly on a farm in Alberta, and later held down several jobs around Toronto, Hamilton, and Buffalo. He finally found a permanent job with the streets department in Toronto in 1926. Longboat was content working outdoors, sweeping the streets and collecting garbage, even if some of his former fans were aghast that he was now doing such unglamorous work. Longboat took pride in the fact that he was able to support his family, even during the Great Depression.

Tom Longboat continued to work for the city of Toronto until a bad back forced him to retire in 1945. With his health failing—he was diagnosed with diabetes in 1946—Longboat moved his family back to the Six Nations Reserve. He died there of pneumonia at the age of sixty-one.

# Archibald Stansfeld
# Belaney ("Grey Owl")
## 1888–1938

I N 1937, Grey Owl crossed the ocean, from Canada to
England, to make a lecture tour. Dressed in deerskins and
moccasins, with his long black hair in braids, he spoke of the
beauty of the natural world and the importance of preserving it.
He showed films of the orphaned beavers he had raised. Throngs
of people who had read his books turned out to see the world's
most famous native North American. Even the King and Queen
invited Grey Owl to give a talk at Buckingham Palace. At the
end of his talk there, the King's eleven-year-old daughter—who
would one day be Queen Elizabeth II—jumped up and begged
for an encore. Grey Owl obliged.

At Grey Owl's lecture in Hastings, though, one woman in the audience was puzzled. She turned to her friend and said, "That's Archie Belaney, or I'll eat my hat." But even she could not imagine the long, strange journey her boyhood friend had taken to become the man on stage.

Archibald Belaney was born in the seaside town of Hastings, England. He rarely saw his father, who left his teenaged mother soon after he was born. From the age of two, Archie was raised by his two unmarried aunts. To escape from their quiet home with its strict rules, the lonely boy spent long hours in the countryside. He loved animals, and he often carried around frogs and mice—even a snake—in his pockets or inside his shirt. He read everything he could find about wood lore and the native people of North America and was determined to see them for himself. Although Archie's aunts tried hard to change his mind, they gave up when he was eighteen, and paid his way to Canada.

Archie Belaney arrived in Halifax in the spring of 1906. He had promised his aunts that he would find a respectable job. However, he lasted only a couple of months as a department store clerk in Toronto. Then he boarded the new Temiskaming and Northern Ontario Railway, and headed north. In the wilderness of Northern Ontario, he learned to canoe and live off the land. He spent most of his time with the Ojibwa (now usually known as Anishinabe) people and left the white world behind. He married an Ojibwa woman named Angele Agwuna and they had a daughter. Her family called Belaney *Was-Sha-Quon-Asin*, the White-Beaked Owl. Later, Belaney liked to translate this name more dramatically, as "He Who Flies By Night." And later still, when he began to write, he signed himself "Grey Owl."

Belaney made his living by trapping animals for their fur pelts. He had, in many ways, the wilderness life he had always dreamed of, but he was restless and unhappy. After three years of marriage, he abandoned his wife and child.

From time to time, Belaney would return to England to visit his aunts, but he never stayed long. During the First World War, he served in the Canadian Army in France. Because of his skills as a marksman, he was made a sniper. When he returned to Canada in 1917, after being wounded in the war, he was more unsettled and moody than ever. He drank too much, and got into fights when he was drunk. By now, he was claiming to some people that he was a native Canadian; he told others that his mother was Apache (a native American people of the American Southwest) and his father was Scottish.

Until he was in his late thirties, this was Belaney's aimless life. Then he met a woman who set him on a new path. Gertrude Bernard was nineteen years old, a well-educated Iroquois who had always lived in the white world. She had a summer job at a resort in Temagami when she met Archie Belaney. She believed him when he told her the Apache-Scottish story. She was enchanted when he gave her an Ojibwa name, Anahareo. Leaving her ordered life and her scholarship at a private girls school, Anahareo joined Belaney in his Temagami cabin.

When winter came, Anahareo begged to go out on the trapline with Belaney. When she finally did, though, she was appalled by the cruelty of leghold animal traps. She challenged Belaney about the brutal way that he made his living. "It is killing your spirit as well as mine," she said. Then she found two young beaver kittens, orphaned when their mother was trapped. She was determined to bring them back to the cabin to raise. The couple named the baby beavers McGinnis and McGinty. Soon, Belaney saw these intelligent and playful animals in a new light. He recalled how he had felt as a child, studying and respecting nature instead of destroying it. As he wrote later, "To kill such creatures seemed monstrous. I would do no more of it."

Belaney now had a practical problem. If he could not earn a living as a trapper, what could he do? He had always kept journals, and his relatives back in England had always enjoyed his letters, full of vivid descriptions of places and people. Now he wrote an essay about McGinnis and McGinty and sent it to an English magazine called *Country Life*. He signed his article "Grey Owl," and led the editors to believe he was a native person. *Country Life* accepted the essay at once, and asked for a book. Belaney responded with *The Men of the Last Frontier*, which became a best-seller in 1931. Soon he was being asked to give lectures about his wilderness experiences. At first he was terrified about speaking in public, but garbed as a native Canadian, in buckskin and braids, he found he had a talent for it. Audiences who were charmed by Grey Owl's stories about McGinnis and McGinty were also receiving an important environmental message. He spoke out about the importance of preserving wilderness areas, and he condemned logging in provincial parks. "You belong to nature," he would remind his listeners. "It does not belong to you."

The Dominion Parks Service (later Parks Canada) soon heard about Grey Owl. They were looking for someone who could promote the national parks system in Canada and in other countries. They gave him and Anahareo a cabin in Riding Mountain National Park in Manitoba and helped him set up a beaver sanctuary. Parks Canada made a series of films about Grey Owl and his new pair of beavers, Jelly Roll and Rawhide (replacements for the "Macs," who had gone missing before the move west). Through these films, he would soon become famous in North America and Britain.

Grey Owl quickly realized that his new home in Manitoba was the wrong place for a beaver sanctuary. In the summer, lake levels fell too low for his beaver colony. In 1932 Parks Canada moved Grey Owl and Anahareo to Lake Ajawan in Prince Albert National Park, Saskatchewan. This time they built a special cabin, called Beaver Lodge, with an entrance for Jelly Roll and Rawhide. Grey Owl wrote three more best-selling books in this cabin. He and Anahareo had a daughter, whom they named Dawn. Although her parents seemed fond of her and often visited her, she was raised by family friends who lived in Prince Albert.

In 1935 Grey Owl made his first tour of England. It was a great success. It also shows just how much audacity he had. In fact, Archie Belaney was returning to his own country. Each time he appeared in public, he risked running into someone he knew.

Belaney had found his calling, but it never made him an easy person to live with. At times he still drank heavily, and he was often bad tempered. Anahareo left him to go prospecting for gold. Although his health was beginning to break down, he agreed to another tour of England in 1937, when he met the Royal Family. He gave two and sometimes three lectures every day, over a three-month period. Although he returned to Canada exhausted, he pushed on with a twelve-week tour of North America in early 1938. Again he drew huge audiences. These were his last public appearances.

In April 1938, two Parks Canada Rangers went to Belaney's remote cabin to check on him. They found him very ill with pneumonia. They bundled him up and took him to hospital in Prince Albert, but he died three days later. He was fifty years old.

For many years, there had been people who knew Grey Owl's real identity. There were native Canadians who saw that he was not really one of them. There were old friends in England who recognized him. There was even a newspaper, the *North Bay Nugget*, which had been given the story in 1937. But everyone, out of liking for Grey Owl or respect for his message, kept his secret—until he died. Within days of his death, a shocked public was reading the story on the front pages. For a time, the fact that Grey Owl was "not really an Indian" overshadowed everything else about him. Today, however, he is recognized as a pioneering conservationist. Although he played a role most of his adult life, no one doubts the sincerity of his environmental message, which is just as important today.

# Norman Bethune

## 1890–1939

NORMAN BETHUNE WAS AN INTELLIGENT, idealistic man. He was also restless, impatient, and tactless. His relatively short life had many twists and turns, as he searched for something truly worthwhile to which he could devote his energies and talents. This quest often put him in harm's way. Twice he volunteered for service in the First World War. Later, he became a famous doctor, inventing or redesigning surgeons' implements. But Norman Bethune's greatest contributions as a doctor came on the battlefields of Spain and China during the 1930s. Today, Canadians remember Norman Bethune as an important doctor. To the Chinese people, he is a revered hero.

Norman Henry Bethune was born in the town of Gravenhurst, Ontario. He was the second of three children born to the Reverend Malcolm Bethune and his wife, Elizabeth. The family moved often while Norman was a boy, and he grew up in several towns across Ontario because his father was posted to different Presbyterian churches. Usually, the family lived in small towns near lakes and forests, and Norman developed a love of the outdoors. He became an excellent swimmer and skater. But his parents had a difficult time keeping their curious, active son out of trouble. They were not always able to control him, but they were able to instill in him the desire to help other people.

The Bethune family was living in the town of Owen Sound when Norman graduated from high school in 1907. Though he was an honours student, Norman decided not to attend university. Instead, he spent a year working as a lumberjack north of Lake Superior. He then spent a year teaching school in a small town outside of Toronto before finally deciding to study science at the University of Toronto in 1909. However, just two years later, he left the University of Toronto to return to the north woods. This time, Norman Bethune had taken a job with Frontier College, a unique adult-education organization that hired people to teach Canadian history and English to men who worked in the wilderness. By day, Bethune would work as a lumberjack; at night, he ran the reading room at a logging camp.

In the fall of 1912, Bethune returned to the University of Toronto to study medicine. He had completed two years of study by the time the First World War began in the summer of 1914. Because Canada was a British colony, the country was at war as soon as England was at war. Bethune was among the many Canadians who volunteered for service in the first few days of the war. He enlisted with the Royal Canadian Army Medical

Corps and was sent to France as a stretcher bearer in February 1915. Bethune's unit was stationed near Ypres during April 1915, when the Canadian Army bravely fought off Germany's poison-gas attacks. As Bethune was carrying a stretcher towards the trenches on April 29, 1915, his left leg was smashed by a fragment from a German bomb. It took him months to recover. The army needed more doctors, so when he was finally healthy again, he was sent back to Toronto to complete his medical studies.

Bethune was part of a University of Toronto medical class that sped through its studies in order to graduate in 1916. One of his classmates was Frederick Banting, who would later gain fame for the discovery of insulin. Bethune returned to the war in 1917, working as a doctor for the British Navy. After the war ended in 1918, Bethune went to London, England, to study pediatrics (children's medicine). He returned to Canada briefly in 1919 but returned to England again in 1920. He married Frances Campbell Penney in London in 1923. The newlyweds came to Canada in 1924, but soon moved to Detroit, in the United States, where Bethune established his first medical practice.

Most of the patients Bethune treated in Detroit were poor; some could not even afford to pay him, and Bethune became troubled by their plight. His skill as a surgeon brought him an increasing number of patients, but his busy work schedule put a strain on his marriage. Then, in the fall of 1926, Bethune was diagnosed with tuberculosis. At this time, before antibiotics, this disease of the lungs was frightening and often deadly. One of the few effective treatments for tuberculosis was rest, fresh air, and a careful diet, so Bethune was sent to a sanatorium at Saranac Lake (a quiet town in the mountains of upper New York state).

During his stay there, Bethune read about a risky surgical technique that could cure him. Though his own doctors advised against it, Bethune had the operation on October 24, 1927. By

Christmas, he was pronounced fit enough to leave the sanatorium, but his illness had changed his outlook on life. "I'm going to find something I can do for the human race," Bethune told one of his fellow patients, "something great, and I am going to do it before I die."

One of the first things Bethune did was move to Montreal to work with Canada's leading expert on tuberculosis, Dr. Edward Archibald. While in Montreal, Bethune wrote many important papers and invented many instruments that were soon being used by thoracic (chest) surgeons across Canada and in other countries. However, Bethune's impatience and quick temper angered many of his fellow doctors. He was critical of them—and of society as well.

He continued to work with the poor in Montreal, and during the Great Depression of the 1930s, Bethune came to believe that the governments of democratic societies should develop publicly funded medical-care and health systems. During a trip to Russia in 1935, Bethune was impressed by the clinics he saw there—the Communist government had set up a system where anyone, regardless of income, could receive free medical care. Bethune hoped to establish a similar system in Canada. He was shocked and disappointed that the Canadian government was not interested, and he decided to become a member of the Communist Party.

Around the same time that the Canadian government was turning down Bethune's health-care proposal, a civil war was breaking out in Spain. Canada was not officially involved in this war, but 1,200 Canadians formed the Mackenzie-Papineau Battalion and went to Spain to help fight for the democratic Spanish Republic against the fascist forces of General Franco. In October of 1936, Norman Bethune also went to Spain to do what he could for the anti-fascist cause. He was offered work as a surgeon in many hospitals there, but Bethune hoped to make a more useful contribution to the war effort. He came up with the idea of a mobile blood-transfusion service. For two months, Bethune and a small group of helpers collected donations of blood from the citizens of Madrid and delivered it to hospitals throughout the Spanish capital. By February and March of 1937, Bethune was delivering blood to medical units at battlefields all over Spain. It was dangerous work, but Bethune's pioneering blood-transfusion system drastically reduced the number of deaths among the wounded. It was the most important medical contribution made during the Spanish Civil War.

In May 1937, Bethune was asked to come back to Canada to make a cross-country speaking tour about the war in Spain. His lectures helped raise much-needed money for humanitarian efforts among the Spanish people. Then, during July of 1937, Japan declared war on China. On January 2, 1938, Bethune left Vancouver on a boat to China. "I refuse to condone . . . the wars which greedy men make against others," he wrote. "Spain and China are part of the same battle. I am going to China because I feel that is where I can be most useful."

In China, Bethune stressed the need for mobile medical units that could attend to soldiers near the battlefields. He travelled the countryside, seeing to the wounded and stopping whenever possible to give treatment to sick peasants. Once, he operated for sixty-nine straight hours (almost three full days!) to attend to the needs of 115 people. Bethune also trained Chinese citizens to provide basic first aid—even to carry out simple surgical procedures—and he established more than twenty teaching and nursing hospitals. Still, conditions were often wretched in the field hospitals, with medicines and bandages in short supply. In October 1939, Bethune was operating on a soldier bare-handed, because there were no surgical gloves. He accidentally cut his own left hand with the scalpel, but did not have time to fix his wound properly. Within a few hours, blood poisoning set in, and on November 12, 1939, Dr. Norman Bethune died. He was already a legend in China, where his picture would later appear on posters and postage stamps. His home country was slower to honour him, but in 1972, Bethune was named a Canadian of "national historic significance." His childhood home in Gravenhurst is now a national museum.

# Agnes Macphail
## 1890–1954

I
N 1921 Agnes Macphail became the first woman in Canada to be elected to the House of Commons. She served as a Member of Parliament until 1940, speaking out on issues that affected farmers, as well as promoting equal rights for women. She was an important supporter of social-welfare programs for the poor, the sick, and the handicapped. Agnes Macphail also believed in prison reform. Her hard work on this issue changed Canadian jails from places where prisoners were treated like slaves to places where lawbreakers could learn to become useful members of society. Yet for all of her good works, Agnes Macphail was often treated as an outsider in Ottawa simply because she was a woman.

Agnes Macphail was born in Proton Township, Grey County, near Georgian Bay in Ontario. (At the time, her family name was spelled Mcphail. She would later change it to its original spelling, after a visit to her family's homeland of Scotland in 1922.) Agnes was the eldest of three daughters born to Dougal and Henrietta Mcphail. Her father, who was a farmer, was well known for his quick wit and powers of persuasion—and Agnes inherited these qualities from him. From her mother, she learned that a strong woman should face trouble and pain without whining or tears. "I owe it to my father that I was elected to Parliament in the first place," Agnes once said, "but I owe it to my mother that I stuck it out once I got there."

Another important influence in Agnes Macphail's life was her mother's mother, Jean Black Campbell. She had been a pioneer in Grey County and taught Agnes to believe that it was the duty of the strong to protect the weak. Agnes would remember these lessons when she got to Ottawa.

Agnes's interest in politics began on the family farm. The Macphails' home was a favourite community meeting place and, as a young girl, Agnes listened as the farmers discussed their crops and the problems they faced. In 1910 Agnes graduated from the Stratford Normal School (teachers college) and began teaching in small country towns across Ontario. As she moved from town to town, she would often live with farming families. Agnes continued to enjoy discussing politics, but she had never become involved in the struggle to win the right for women to vote. However, when women were finally given the right to vote in federal elections in 1918, and then given the right to run for office in 1919, she became actively involved in politics. It turned out that Macphail was entering politics at a time when the Canadian system was undergoing a lot of change.

During the First World War and the years immediately after,

there was considerable social and political unrest in Canada. Canadian farmers had been among those who strongly opposed Conscription (a plan to draft men between the ages of twenty and forty-five into the army) because young men were needed to work in the fields. Farmers had been expected to produce as much as they could for the war effort. Many of them had spent a lot of money to buy more land and better equipment. However, demand for their crops dropped quickly when the war ended. The prices they could charge came down just as quickly, so that many farmers found themselves deeply in debt. Farmers all across the country were unhappy with the way the political parties had treated them, and so they organized new parties. In 1919 a party called the United Farmers of Ontario actually won the provincial election. Farmer candidates would also do well in the Manitoba elections of 1920, and in 1921 the United Farmers of Alberta would win the election there.

Not surprisingly, Agnes Macphail became involved with the United Farmers of Ontario (known as the UFO). She joined a group called the United Farm Women of Ontario and began to attend UFO meetings. She even wrote a column for the *Farmer's Sun* newspaper. During the Ontario election of 1919, she spoke frequently on behalf of UFO candidates.

In December of 1920, a new national party—called the Progressive Party—was formed. For the Canadian general election of 1921, the Progressive Party obtained the support of the provincial farm parties. When the United Farmers of Ontario voted to select candidates for the 1921 election, Agnes Macphail was one of ten people hoping to get the nomination in the riding of South-East Grey (later Grey-Bruce). She was the only woman running, and it was considered a big surprise when she defeated the nine men. Some party members demanded that Macphail withdraw so that a man could become the candidate, but she refused. In the election that followed, the Progressives won more votes than any party except the Liberals, and Agnes Macphail won in her riding. She was one of five women who had run in the election of 1921, but she was the only one to win.

On Agnes's first day in the House of Commons she discovered a bouquet of roses waiting at her desk—only to find out they had been left by a man who had lost a bet! From the beginning, resentful male colleagues let her know that they felt being a Member of Parliament was improper behaviour for a woman. Some would rudely walk out of the House of Commons whenever she got up to speak. Others would act in an excessively polite way, to make her feel like an outsider. In the hallways of the House of Commons, people would stop to stare at her. She was made to feel so uncomfortable in the House dining room that she lost twelve pounds during her first few months in office and took to eating in downtown Ottawa restaurants instead.

Despite her problems, Macphail won re-election in 1925. Even though the Progressive Party collapsed a short time after that, she continued to win re-election as an Independent candidate until 1940. Still, as the only woman in the House of Commons until 1935, Agnes Macphail found that "I couldn't open my mouth to say the simplest thing without it appearing in the newspapers." Making matters worse, the coverage she received in the newspapers was decidedly unfair. Reporters picked on the clothes she wore, including the fact that she did not like to wear a hat (which was considered unladylike). Because she was not married, she was portrayed as "a cantankerous old maid." Yet the truth was that she had chosen not to get married because she felt that most men treated their wives unfairly. Macphail believed in equality between men and women, both "economically and morally," and felt it would be wrong to get married until this was achieved. Later in life, when she handed over her papers to the

National Archives of Canada, she made sure to include a few love letters. Those who knew her well had always known that she was friendly and fun-loving, despite what the newspapers said.

During her nineteen years as a Member of Parliament, Agnes Macphail worked hard to ensure that farmers got a fair deal from the government. She supported such issues as crop-failure insurance for farmers, unemployment insurance for workers, medical insurance, family allowances for the poor, and old-age pensions for the elderly. She would become best known for her efforts on behalf of prison reform, drawing the attention of Parliament to Canada's dirty, rat-infested jails, where whippings and beatings were commonplace. Throughout the 1930s, she spoke out against war. Though she was not opposed when Canada entered the Second World War in 1939, her pacifist views likely contributed to her defeat during the election of 1940.

After leaving the House of Commons, Macphail continued to support the farmers through a newspaper column on agricultural issues in the *Globe and Mail*. She returned to politics in 1943, when she and Rae Luckock became the first two women elected to the Ontario legislature. Macphail was now a member of the Co-operative Commonwealth Federation, forerunner of the New Democratic Party (the NDP). She was defeated in the provincial election of 1945, but was re-elected for a final time in 1948 before losing again in 1951. Her political career was now over, although many people believed she would have made an excellent senator. Agnes Macphail died in 1954, after suffering her third heart attack. She was sixty-three years old.

On the 100th anniversary of Macphail's birth, on March 24, 1990, the Ontario NDP Women's Committee established the Agnes Macphail Award to honour women who make a significant contribution to the advancement of women and women's issues.

# Frederick Banting

## 1891–1941

APPROXIMATELY 2 MILLION PEOPLE in Canada (about one out of every fifteen people) suffer from diabetes. This disease affects the body's ability to convert sugar and starch into the materials needed to help a person remain healthy. Some children are diagnosed with diabetes; more often, it is a disease that develops in adults. Although there is still no cure, most people who suffer from diabetes today can control the disease with diet and exercise. When this is not sufficient, diabetics can be treated with insulin.

Before the discovery of insulin, children diagnosed with diabetes usually died within a few years. Some adult diabetics could live longer, by eating as little sugar and starch as possible. Unfortunately, this meant that most diabetics faced the choice of either dying quickly from their disease or more slowly from starvation. No wonder the discovery of insulin by Dr. Frederick Banting in 1922 was hailed as a miracle.

Frederick Grant Banting was born in Alliston, Ontario, north of Toronto, and raised on the family farm. The youngest of six children, Fred had plenty of chores to do, and this may have affected his school work. He was not an outstanding student, but he did work very hard. Although he had to repeat some of his exams in order to graduate from high school, his final marks were good enough to gain admission to the University of Toronto.

Banting considered becoming a teacher, though his parents hoped he would study to become a minister. In his second year at the University of Toronto, he decided he would study medicine. It was likely that this had been his goal all along, ever since witnessing a terrible accident as a boy in Alliston. Young Fred had seen two workers fall off the roof of a house, and he was part of the crowd that stayed with them until the doctor arrived. "I watched every movement of his skillful hands," Banting would later recall, "and in those tense minutes I thought, 'the greatest service to man is in the medical profession.' From that day on, it was my greatest ambition to become a doctor."

In the summer of 1914, Banting was preparing to return to the University of Toronto for his third year of medical school. But his plans would soon change. The First World War began on August 4, 1914, and the very next day Banting tried to enlist in the Canadian Army. He was turned down because of his poor eyesight. In the spring of 1915, he tried again to enlist. This time he was accepted into the Royal Canadian Army Medical Corps. Banting was not supposed to graduate from the University of

Toronto until 1917, but since the army needed doctors, the entire U of T medical class worked through the summer of 1916. Banting wrote his final exams in October and graduated on December 9, 1916. He reported to the army the following day. Lieutenant Banting then set sail for England, where he was posted to a Canadian hospital.

Banting was later promoted to the rank of captain and transferred for service in France. He served with distinction and bravery in France, receiving the Military Cross for his actions on September 28, 1918. Banting suffered a serious wound that day while attending to other wounded soldiers, but continued to treat the other soldiers for another seventeen hours before getting help for himself.

Banting returned to Canada after the war and worked briefly at Toronto's Hospital for Sick Children to complete his medical training. In June 1920, he moved to London, Ontario, and opened his own medical practice there. As a new doctor in town, Banting found it hard to attract patients. In the month of July, for example, he earned just four dollars. He had to sell his car to help make ends meet.

In October 1920, Banting was offered a teaching position in the medical school at the University of Western Ontario in London. One of his earliest jobs was to give a lecture on how the body used sugar and other carbohydrates to produce energy. While preparing for this lecture, Banting became fascinated by the research being done on diabetes. Other researchers had already figured out that diabetes was caused by problems in the pancreas (an organ just beneath the stomach). The pancreas is supposed to produce a protein called insulin, which helps the body digest sugar. People with diabetes do not produce this protein. Doctors believed that if they could find a way to replace the missing insulin, they could treat people with diabetes. But no one had been able to find a way to remove insulin from a healthy pancreas and give it to people who were diabetic.

Banting had almost no experience with medical research, but he came up with a plan to produce insulin that he thought would work. Dr. J.R.R. Macleod of the University of Toronto was one of the top scientists working on diabetes, and Banting was able to interest Macleod in his theory. On May 17, 1921, Banting was given a small lab in Toronto and a twenty-one-year-old assistant, a recent U of T biochemistry graduate named Charles Best. Together, Banting and Best experimented on dogs. During the summer of 1921, they found that they could keep a diabetic dog alive for three weeks using insulin they had produced in the pancreas of another dog. After months of work, and with help from Macleod, they found that they could also keep dogs alive using insulin from cows. Later, Dr. James Collip helped Banting and Best find ways to improve the insulin they were creating. Sometimes, Banting thought Collip was competing with him, and sometimes he thought Macleod was claiming too much credit for their work, but together they came up with an insulin extract they could use on people. The first successful test was made on a human being in January 1922. Leonard Thompson, a fourteen-year-old boy near death from diabetes, was restored to health by regular doses of insulin. Reports on the success of insulin created worldwide interest almost overnight.

Soon diabetic patients were flocking to Toronto. Long lines of people made thin by the disease waited patiently outside a small medical office that Banting had set up. He treated people for very low fees, saying that "insulin doesn't belong to me; it belongs to the world."

Dr. Frederick Banting was later knighted (1934) by King George V of England for his discovery of insulin, but in 1923 he and Dr. Macleod shared the Nobel Prize for Medicine. Banting was upset that Charles Best did not share the award, so Banting gave him half his $20,000 prize money. Macleod shared his prize money with James Collip.

In addition to providing a life-saving treatment for diabetics, Dr. Frederick Banting's achievements with insulin helped make people realize the importance of scientific research. The University of Toronto created the Banting Research Foundation and the Banting Institute. Banting himself donated much of his Nobel Prize money to research. He could have become rich from the discovery of insulin, but he sold his patent to the University of Toronto for just $1. He wanted the U of T's Connaught Laboratories to be able to make as much insulin as was needed for as little cost as possible.

During his days as a struggling doctor in London, Ontario, Banting had taken up painting as a way to relax. He became quite good at it. In 1927 Banting met A.Y. Jackson, one of the Group of Seven, and they became good friends. While Banting continued to work as a medical researcher into the 1930s, he joked with Jackson that he would retire and take up painting full-time when he turned fifty. Sadly, he did not live that long. When the Second World War broke out in 1939, Banting volunteered to do wartime research. On February 21, 1941, on a flight from Canada to England, his plane crashed in the bush north of Gander, Newfoundland. Only the pilot survived. He later told of how Banting tried his best to treat the other passengers, until he died of his injuries the following day. Dr. Frederick Banting was only forty-nine years old.

# Wilfrid Reid "Wop" May

## 1896–1952

I N DECEMBER 1928, a diphtheria epidemic threatened the town of Little Red River, a tiny settlement in the wilderness of northern Alberta. An employee of the Hudson's Bay Company had died of the dreaded throat disease on December 15, and other cases were breaking out. Anti-diphtheria serum was needed desperately or the entire community of 300 people might fall ill. The town doctor rushed to nearby Fort Vermillion to dispatch a messenger to the closest telegraph station. It took the messenger twelve days to reach Peace River by horse and dogsled, but the message was finally received by Dr. Malcolm Bow, deputy minister of the department of health, in Edmonton.

Dr. Bow realized that it would take at least two weeks to deliver the anti-diphtheria medicine to Little Red River by train and dog sled. He needed someone who could transport the medicine by plane, if it was to arrive in time to save the town. Dr. Bow asked pilot Wilfrid May if such a flight could be made in temperatures of –30 degrees Celsius. May believed it could, and volunteered to deliver the serum. By this time, he already had plenty of experience as a bush pilot, flying miners and supplies in and out of the uncharted Canadian northland. But May had never made a flight like this one.

The only airplane available to May and his co-pilot, Vic Horner, was a tiny two-seater with a 75-horsepower engine. It had no skis for a proper winter landing. Worse yet, the airplane had an open cockpit, meaning May and Horner would be exposed to the bone-chilling temperatures and the bitter, biting wind. The pilots took off from Edmonton on January 2, 1929, but a blizzard forced them to land halfway through their 600-kilometre journey. They had to wait until the next day to continue their mercy flight. By the time they finally arrived at Fort Vermillion on the afternoon of January 3, May and Horner were so badly chilled and frostbitten that they had to be carried out of the cockpit. But the precious serum they had carried was safe, and the tiny town was saved.

When news reached Edmonton that the pilots were on their way back home, thousands of people gathered at the airfield to greet them. It was not the first time that "Wop" May had been hailed as a hero. Nor would it be the last.

Wilfrid May was the youngest of three children born to Alexander and Elizabeth May in the town of Carberry, Manitoba. The child was named after the new prime minister of Canada, Wilfrid Laurier, who had been elected in the same year as the baby's birth—1896. The family moved to Edmonton in

1902, and around that same time, a visiting cousin had difficulty in pronouncing Wilfrid's name correctly. She called him "Woppie," and the nickname caught on with the family. Later, it was shorted to "Wop."

Alexander May had sold farm tools in Carberry, then operated a service station in Edmonton. He sold gasoline and tires and became an expert in repairing automobiles, which were just beginning to become popular. Wilfrid and his older brother, Court, grew up around machines and came to love the speed and risk of racing. In 1910 they witnessed a demonstration of the first airplane to fly in Alberta, and from that moment, both brothers wanted to be pilots. At Victoria High School in Edmonton, Wop May met another boy who loved airplanes. His name was Arthur Roy Brown.

After the outbreak of the First World War in 1914, the May brothers learned that some of the soldiers who had volunteered for the Canadian Army had been able to join England's Royal Flying Corps (later known as the Royal Air Force). They hoped to do the same, but Court had had polio as a child. His only lasting disability from the disease was a weakness in one leg, but this was enough to make him ineligible for military service. Wilfrid, however, enlisted with the 202nd City of Edmonton Battalion in 1916. He applied for a transfer to the Royal Flying Corps shortly after his arrival in England, and he was finally accepted late in 1917. May graduated as a pilot in March 1918 and was sent to France to join the 209th Squadron the following month. His flight commander there was none other than his high-school friend Roy Brown.

Brown was, by then, an experienced flyer who had been in combat since 1915. He advised May to stay out of the action during his first few missions and to observe the fighting patterns from a distance. However, during his third flight, on April 21, 1918,

May spotted a German plane he believed he could attack. What he didn't know was that while he was chasing this plane, he himself was being chased by the greatest of all First World War aces—Manfred von Richthofen. The "Red Baron," as he was known, had already shot down eighty planes. May might well have become the German's eighty-first victim if not for his friend Roy Brown. Brown dived towards the Baron's red Fokker triplane, with his guns blazing. It has never been certain whether the fatal shot came from Brown or from the gun of an Australian soldier on the ground, but the Red Baron crashed and died of his wounds. Spared from his own brush with death, May went on to become a skilled fighter pilot. He shot down thirteen planes during the final six months of the war and received the Distinguished Flying Cross from King George V of England.

In the spring of 1919, many ex-soldiers and pilots were having trouble finding work back home. Wop May and his brother, Court, decided to buy their own airplane and form the May Airplanes Company. Much of their early work involved the younger May doing stunt flights at fairs across Western Canada and the United States. One of his first jobs was flying the mayor of Edmonton over the local baseball stadium to throw out the first pitch of the 1919 season. But important work was slow to come. The first big job came in 1921, when May and another pilot were hired to fly two planes from New York to Edmonton for the Imperial Oil Company. Still, the brothers were having trouble making enough money. Then came a tragic loss: Court May's weak leg gave out on a flight of stairs. He had a terrible fall and died of his injuries.

May left the flying business following his brother's death. Soon after, he met a woman named Vi Bode and married her in 1924. Now he needed a job, and found one as a mechanic for the National Cash Register Company. Unfortunately, he suffered a serious injury on the job when a steel splinter flew off his lathe and into his eye. The accident left him partially blind and would eventually end his flying career.

However, in the late 1920s, there were suddenly many more jobs for experienced pilots. Even with his eye injury, May and other bush pilots, including "Punch" Dickins and Harold Oaks, were able to find plenty of work delivering airmail and other supplies to communities across the Canadian North. In 1927 May founded the Edmonton Flying Club, which was the first flying club in Canada, and in 1929 he was awarded the McKee Trophy (for contributions to Canadian aviation) for his mercy flight to Fort Vermillion. In 1932 he used his plane to help the RCMP track down a criminal known as the "Mad Trapper," who was on the loose in the Northwest Territories. May was made an Officer of the Order of the British Empire (OBE) for his many contributions to Canadian aviation in 1935, but by 1936 his damaged eye had to be removed. His pilot's licence was revoked, but May continued to work in administrative jobs for a Canadian airline company.

After the Second World War began in 1939, Canada and England reached an agreement that saw Canada become the home to an ambitious, Empire-wide, flight-training program: the British Commonwealth Air Training Plan. Wop May helped set up the program and supervised one of the schools in Edmonton. He also developed and trained a parachute squad that volunteered with Canadian and American forces. This squad helped save the lives of many downed airmen. After the war, he continued to work with Canadian Airways until he collapsed and died while on vacation with his son, Denny, in 1952. In 1974 Wilfrid Reid "Wop" May was named one of the original members of the Canadian Aviation Hall of Fame.

# Lionel Conacher
## 1900–1954

LIONEL CONACHER WAS BORN on a day of celebration and would grow up to become the most celebrated athlete of his time. On May 24, 1900, Canadians were honouring the birthday of Queen Victoria, then in her sixty-third year as the ruler of the British Empire. Just before Conacher's own birth, the British Army, fighting the Boer War in South Africa, had marched into Pretoria, the Boer capital. Ben and Elizabeth Conacher chose to name their new child Lionel Pretoria, after the site of the important British victory.

Lionel Conacher was his family's oldest boy, and the third of their ten children, who grew up poor in a working-class neighbourhood of Toronto. He attended Jesse Ketchum School, where the principal believed that playing organized sports helped keep children out of trouble. Soon it seemed that every child in the neighbourhood was playing football, lacrosse, or hockey (depending on the season) on the fields at Jesse Ketchum Park. Young Lionel quickly came to realize that success in athletics offered him his best chance to escape poverty.

Though he had to leave school after grade 8 to begin working with his father, Lionel Conacher continued to make time for sports. When he was fourteen, he helped his football team win the Toronto city championship. At age sixteen, he won the Ontario 125-pound wrestling championship. He took up hockey for the first time that year, and by 1920 he had helped the Parkdale Canoe Club hockey team win the Memorial Cup (Canadian junior championship). That same year he also won the Canadian light-heavyweight boxing championship.

Conacher seemed to excel at every sport he tried, but football was his favourite. In 1921 he joined the Toronto Argonauts. Football in that era was very different from the game of today. The most notable difference was that forward passing was against the rules. Teams had to rely on strong runners and good kickers, and no one was better in either skill than Lionel Conacher. Now standing six foot, one inch (183 cm) and weighing 195 pounds (88 kg), Conacher was bigger than most athletes of his time. He was strong enough to power through tackles, yet he was also fast enough to outrun almost everyone. His combination of strength and speed led sportswriters to call him "The Big Train."

In his first game for the Argonauts in September 1921, Conacher scored 23 of his team's 27 points. The Argos went on to win all six games they played in the regular season, then posted two more victories in the playoffs to reach the Grey Cup championship. Playing against the Edmonton Eskimos, Conacher rushed for two touchdowns (then worth five points each), kicked a field goal, and punted for a pair of singles. In all, he collected 15 points to lead the Argos to a 23–0 victory. With the outcome well in hand in the fourth quarter, Conacher left the game early. He had to rush off to join his hockey team, which had a big game that evening! Later in his sports career, Conacher would drive in the winning run in the bottom of the last inning to give his Hillcrest baseball team the championship, then jump in a car and drive across town to play with the Toronto Maitlands lacrosse team. The Maitlands were losing when he got there, but Conacher rallied the team to victory.

In the early 1920s, Lionel Conacher was the most famous athlete in Canada, but he could not accept money to play or he would lose his amateur status. Hockey teams like the Toronto St. Patricks (who would later become the Maple Leafs) and the Montreal Canadiens were offering large contracts if he would join the NHL. If Conacher did that, though, he would not be allowed to play the other sports he loved. Still, even if Conacher could not take money to play, there were other ways to earn a living from sports. Owners of the teams he joined were happy to find him good jobs in their companies. When Conacher discovered that his name on a sign was enough to attract customers, he opened his own clothes-cleaning business. Later, he and his brother Charlie (a famous hockey player for the Toronto Maple Leafs) operated a gas station in the neighbourhood where they had grown up.

In 1923 Conacher left Toronto for Pittsburgh, Pennsylvania, where he had the opportunity to play college football in the United States. He also joined the Pittsburgh Yellow Jackets hockey team and led them to the United States amateur championship in 1924 and 1925. When Pittsburgh was offered an NHL franchise for the 1925–26 season, Conacher finally agreed to become a professional. He and all his Yellow Jackets teammates signed with the new club. But it wasn't enough just to become a pro in hockey. In the spring of 1926, Conacher signed with the Toronto Maple Leafs baseball team in the Triple-A International League (the highest minor league below the American League and National League). He was only a part-time player, but he attracted big crowds to the ballpark and helped Toronto win the Little World Series.

As a hockey player, Conacher was not a great skater, but he could shoot hard and he was excellent at blocking opponents' shots. Through determined effort, he made himself into an all-star defenceman—and he kept right on playing other sports. In the summer of 1931, he joined a professional lacrosse league with several other NHL hockey players. Before that year, lacrosse had always been played outdoors, on fields similar to those used for soccer, but the new pro league played the game inside hockey arenas. Conacher's team won the championship.

During the summer of 1932, Conacher wrestled as a pro across Canada, and before the hockey season began in 1933, he organized a professional football team. The team was called the Chefs because it was owned by a Toronto food company called Crosse and Blackwell. The Chefs had to play their games against American teams because Canadian football was still strictly amateur. Conacher played on the team with his brother Charlie. In 1934 they both joined a new football team called the Aromints, which was owned by the Wrigley Chewing Gum Company.

During all this time, Lionel Conacher was still playing hockey. Earlier in 1934, he had won the Stanley Cup with the Chicago Blackhawks. In 1935 he won it again, this time as a member of the Montreal Maroons. In September of 1936,

Conacher wrote an article about his sports career for *Maclean's* magazine. In it, he spoke of his many injuries: nose broken eight times, a broken leg, a broken arm, several broken bones in his hands, ten cracked ribs, two knee operations, and 650 stitches (some 500 or so to his face and head). After the hockey season of 1936–37, he decided it was time to retire.

Now out of sports, Conacher was convinced by members of the Liberal Party to enter politics. In the Ontario election of 1937, he was elected as a Member of Provincial Parliament for the Toronto riding of Bracondale, which included his childhood home. These were the days of the Great Depression, and Conacher worked hard to help the poor people of his riding. When the Second World War began in 1939, Lionel Conacher was made an honourary squadron leader in the Royal Canadian Air Force. He was also recruited by the federal government to help organize a sports program for the Canadian armed forces.

After the war ended, Conacher entered federal politics. In 1954, when he was in Ottawa playing in the annual softball game between Members of Parliament and newspaper reporters, he hit a long fly ball into left field and raced to third base for a triple. Suddenly, he collapsed. Shockingly, Canada's greatest athlete had died of a heart attack.

That Lionel Conacher was indeed Canada's greatest athlete had been confirmed just a few years before his death. In 1950 he had easily topped a Canadian Press poll as Canada's Top Athlete of the Half-Century. After his death, Conacher was elected to the Canadian Sports Hall of Fame, the Canadian Football Hall of Fame, the Lacrosse Hall of Fame, and the Hockey Hall of Fame. When a new poll was conducted in 2000 to name Canada's greatest athlete of the entire century, Lionel Conacher still managed to finish fourth in the voting even though he had been dead for forty-six years.

# Howie Morenz

## 1902–1937

HOWIE MORENZ TURNED FIFTEEN in 1917, the year that his family moved from the tiny town of Mitchell, Ontario, to nearby Stratford. That fall, he decided to try out for the Stratford Midgets hockey team. The Midgets were a junior team, which meant that the upper age limit was twenty. Many of the boys on the team were much older than Howie, and some of them had played on the team the year before, when they won the Northern Hockey League championship. Howie arrived at practice with only his stick and skates. He was battered and bruised by the older boys and left the ice with his hands bleeding.

Hockey had been so much easier in Mitchell. As the youngest in a family with six children, Howie had followed his two older brothers out onto the backyard rink, and then onto the pond where the Thames River was dammed. He was ten years younger than his oldest brother, Wilfred, and six years younger than Ezra, but playing with older children helped Howie develop his hockey sense and his blazing speed. By the time he was fourteen, he had helped Mitchell win the Western Ontario Juvenile District hockey championship. And despite the rough start, he would soon be winning titles in Stratford, too.

After his first practice in his new hometown, Howie Morenz told Father Bill Gerby, who ran the team, that he would not be coming out anymore. However, when the Stratford Midgets were beaten 25–3 in their first game of the season, the star from Mitchell was invited to try again. This time he made the team. He played his first game on January 1, 1918, and helped Stratford to an 8–2 victory. Morenz played centre. He had one goal and helped both his wingers score three times each. He also recorded several penalties. Unfortunately, the victory marked Stratford's only win during their four-game schedule with the Ontario Hockey Association. The team did much better, though, in its games in the Northern Hockey League. In fact, Stratford went all the way to the league final. In the championship game, Morenz sped everywhere on the ice, scoring six times as the Midgets romped to a 15–0 win.

Howie Morenz had left school behind when he left Mitchell. Since he had never been a good student, it seemed much more practical to learn a trade than to continue his formal education. Like his father and his uncle, Morenz got a job in the machine shop of the Grand Trunk Railway, and worked as a machinist's apprentice. In addition, he played shortstop on the company baseball team in summertime. By the winter of 1918–19, Morenz was playing hockey with three different teams: the Grand Trunk "Trunkers," the Stratford Midgets, and the Stratford Indians.

By the end of his sixth season in Stratford (1922–23), Morenz's teams had won nine different championships. The Midgets had reached the finals of the Memorial Cup (Canadian junior championship) in 1921, but the most important title, in terms of Howie's future in hockey, was the 1923 railway championship. Cecil Hart of the Montreal Canadiens had seen Morenz score all three goals in a 3–2 victory over a Montreal railway team in a game at the Mount Royal Arena. In early June of 1923, Canadiens owner Leo Dandurand found out that the Toronto St. Patricks (forerunners of the Maple Leafs) were trying to sign Morenz for their team. He sent Hart to Stratford to get Morenz's signature on a Montreal contract instead.

On July 7, 1923, Howie Morenz signed a contract with the Canadiens. The deal would reportedly pay him $2,500 for the 1923–24 season, plus a bonus of $850. At the time, this was considered a very good contract. But in August of 1923, Morenz sent the contract and his bonus cheque back to Leo Dandurand. He said that he had changed his mind; he could not leave his family or his job in Stratford. He was actually worried that he was too small and too light, and that he wouldn't be good enough to play in the National Hockey League. Dandurand convinced Morenz to attend the Canadiens training camp in December (NHL seasons were much shorter then) and see what happened. After his first workout with the team on December 4, 1923, the Montreal *Gazette* reported that Morenz was "a likely prospect." After the next day's scrimmage games, the papers said his play was "outstanding." By the time the season started on December 15, Howie Morenz was the starting centre for the Montreal Canadiens.

At this point in hockey history, a starting player on a hockey team would be expected to play at least 45 to 50 minutes of a

60-minute game. Top stars might never get off the ice for a rest. Playing on a line with Aurel Joliat and Billy Boucher, Howie Morenz saw plenty of ice time. He finished the twenty-four-game NHL season with thirteen goals, which ranked him among the league leaders. The Canadiens finished in second place, but they beat the Ottawa Senators in the playoffs to win the NHL championship. In those days, the Stanley Cup did not belong only to the NHL, so the Canadiens had to face challengers from the Pacific Coast Hockey Association and the Western Canada Hockey League. Morenz scored four goals in four games as Montreal beat teams from Vancouver and Calgary to win the Stanley Cup.

Good as he'd been as a rookie, Howie Morenz was even better in 1924–25. The NHL season expanded to thirty games that year and he scored twenty-eight times. Linemate Aurel Joliat had thirty goals. The Canadiens again reached the Stanley Cup finals, but this time they lost to the Victoria Cougars, who became the last non-NHL team ever to win the prized trophy.

The 1924–25 season was important to the NHL because the league had expanded into the United States for the first time. The Boston Bruins joined up that year, and they would soon be followed by teams in New York, Chicago, Detroit, and Pittsburgh. Star players like Howie Morenz had helped make the Canadian sport popular in the United States. In fact, American reporters began to call Morenz "the Babe Ruth of Hockey" because of his great skill and because so many fans came to arenas just to see him play. His many other nicknames came from his amazing skating speed: "The Canadien Comet," "The Hurtling Habitant," "The Mitchell Meteor," and "The Stratford Streak."

Morenz was the biggest star in hockey during the colourful days of the late 1920s and early 1930s. He was the NHL's top scorer in 1927–28 and 1930–31, and he won the Hart Trophy as the league's most valuable player in 1928, 1931, and 1932. He also helped the Canadiens win the Stanley Cup again in both 1930 and 1931. But then he began to slow down. He'd been an aggressive player throughout his career, but injuries were catching up with him. He was traded to the Chicago Blackhawks in 1934, then dealt to the New York Rangers during the 1935–36 season.

Montreal got Morenz back for the 1936–37 season, and at first he was playing like his old self again. Then, in a game against Chicago on January 28, 1937, misfortune struck. With the Canadiens leading 4–1, Morenz sped into the Blackhawks end. Defenceman Earl Siebert checked him as he tried to go around the net. Morenz fell, and his left skate stuck into the wooden boards. When Siebert fell over top of him, the bone in his left leg shattered.

From his hospital bed, Morenz talked bravely of coming back from the injury, but the constant stream of guests and well-wishers in his room sapped his body of strength. Weeks later, he was still in the hospital. On March 8, 1937, Howie Morenz collapsed and died. The official cause of death was listed as heart failure.

On March 10, 1937, a funeral was held at the Montreal Forum. Over 10,000 fans attended the service, and thousands more lined the streets outside. The NHL played an All-Star Game to raise money for the Morenz family on November 2, 1937, and in 1945, Howie Morenz was one of the first twelve men inducted into the Hockey Hall of Fame. In 1950 he was voted Canada's Greatest Hockey Player of the Half-Century. To this day, "The Stratford Streak" is still considered to be one of the all-time greats of the game.

# Bobbie Rosenfeld
## 1904–1969

I F BOBBIE ROSENFELD was not already the most famous female athlete in Canada before the 1928 Amsterdam Olympics, she certainly was afterwards. There, she won a gold and a silver medal. She also impressed everyone with her sportsmanship when she helped a Canadian teammate to the finish line, even though it may have cost her another Olympic medal for herself. Bobbie Rosenfeld's skill as a sprinter led the Canadian women's track-and-field team to the top finish at the 1928 Olympics, but this was only a small part of her athletic achievement. In addition to starring in several track-and-field events, she won many basketball, baseball, and hockey championships—and, once, Toronto's tennis title. It was said that the easiest way to sum up her athletic ability was to point out that the only sport at which she did not excel was swimming.

Bobbie Rosenfeld (whose real name was Fanny) was born in Russia at a time when life for Jews in that country was particularly difficult. They faced not only discrimination but also organized forms of violence known as "pogroms." Fanny's family left Russia for Canada when she was still a baby, and she grew up in the small town of Barrie, Ontario. According to family stories, she ran her first race out of necessity. She and her sister had lost the lunch they brought to a town picnic. Fortunately, a race had been organized for children, with a box lunch as a prize. Fanny entered and won.

Soon, Fanny became one of the best-known young athletes in Barrie, leading her high-school basketball team to a league title while also starring in her favourite sport, hockey. Word got around that she could also run as fast as any boy, but she had trouble finding anyone to challenge her after beating some of the male runners at Barrie Collegiate. Her first major trophy came at the Great War Veterans Association track meet in Barrie in 1922. By then she was cutting her hair short, so that it would not get in her eyes when she competed. Her short, bobbed hairstyle led to the nickname "Bobbie."

In this era, people felt it was unladylike for women to compete at sports. Nevertheless, the Toronto Ladies Athletic Club had been founded in 1920, and the city had a thriving women's sports scene. In 1922 the Rosenfeld family moved to Toronto. With her parents' encouragement, Rosenfeld became as dominant in the big city as she had been in her small hometown. Soon she was playing guard for the Lakesides women's basketball team, playing centre for the North Toronto Ladies hockey team, and starring as shortstop for the Hinde and Dauche softball club. Her big break came when her softball team was playing at a sports carnival in Beaverton, Ontario. The day's main event was a women's 100-yard dash, and Bobbie's teammates persuaded her to enter the race. Not only did she win, she beat the reigning Canadian 100-yard champion, Rosa Grosse.

Rosenfeld's win in Beaverton earned her a chance to run in her first major track meet at the 1923 Canadian National Exhibition. She would face Rosa Grosse again, and would also race against world record holder Helen Fikley of Chicago. However, Rosenfeld did not have the proper sportswear. "I hunted all over town," she later recalled. "I finished wearing my brother's swimming trunks, my dad's socks, and a gym jersey." Though she may have looked strange, Rosenfeld not only won the 100-yard dash, but also teamed up with Grosse and two other Toronto runners to defeat the Chicago relay team. As she crossed the finish line, she spotted her father sitting on the stadium fence, banging on the wood and shouting, "Dat's my goil!" Later that day, Rosenfeld helped the Hinde and Dauche softball team win the city championship. A year later, she won the Toronto tennis championship.

As great an athlete as she was, there was no way for any woman to make a living from sports in the 1920s. Bobbie Rosenfeld worked as a stenographer (secretary) at the Patterson Candy chocolate factory in Toronto. However, as her fame as an athlete grew, the Patterson company decided to form its own sports club. The Patterson Athletic Club finished third at the 1925 Ontario Ladies Track and Field Championship—a remarkable feat because Bobbie Rosenfeld was the only member of the team! In just one day of competition, she finished first in the 220-yard race, the 120-yard hurdles, the long jump, the discus, and the shot put, while adding a second-place finish in the 100-yard dash. Not surprisingly, she was awarded a trophy as the all-around female athlete of the year.

Bobbie Rosenfeld was well on her way to becoming Canada's most famous female athlete, and she would soon be as well known as any male athlete in the country. The International Amateur Athletic Federation decided to allow women to compete in track-and-field events at the Olympics for the first time in 1928. At the trials to select the country's first women's Olympic team, Rosenfeld set Canadian records in the long jump and the discus and was just 4/5ths of a second off the world record in the 100-metre dash. Not surprisingly, she made the team, along with fellow runners Jane Bell, Myrtle Cook, Ethel Smith, and Jean Thompson, plus high-jumper Ethel Catherwood. The Canadian Press would soon dub these women "The Matchless Six."

Rosenfeld was supposed to compete in the discus and the 100-metre race at the Amsterdam Olympics, but when both events were scheduled on the same day, she chose to skip the discus. Three false starts marred the 100-metre race, which also saw fellow Canadian Myrtle Cook disqualified. When the race finally began, Rosenfeld was slow out of the blocks. American Betty Robinson took the early lead, but the Canadian champion was coming up fast. When they crossed the finish line they were so close together it was impossible to tell for sure who had won. Eventually the judges decided that Robinson had been the winner, with Rosenfeld taking the silver. Ethel Smith won the bronze. The Canadians got their revenge in the 4-x-100-metre relay, when Rosenfeld, Smith, Cook, and Bell raced to victory over the American team. Yet Rosenfeld's finest Olympic moment may have been her fifth-place finish in the 800-metre race.

Rosenfeld had never trained for this event; she entered the race only to give encouragement to Jean Thompson.

(Thompson had suffered a leg injury and Canadian officials worried it would affect her performance.) With Rosenfeld urging her on, Thompson had a good chance to win the silver medal, until she was accidentally bumped by another runner and slipped back to fourth place. Rosenfeld was in ninth place at the time, but she sprinted to catch up with Thompson. Many who watched the race believed Rosenfeld could have continued to sprint towards a medal. However, she stayed just behind Thompson, urging her on to her best possible finish. In the end, Thompson could do no better than fourth. Rosenfeld was fifth, but her selfless actions earned her more accolades than any medal could have.

A crowd of 200,000 people turned out in Toronto to welcome home Bobbie Rosenfeld and the Canadian women's team. She was now at the height of her fame. Unknown to anyone, however, her career was all but over. In 1929 Rosenfeld was struck with a severe form of arthritis. The pain in her ankles was so excruciating that doctors discussed amputating one of her feet. However, after eight months of bedrest and a year on crutches, she was back playing both hockey and baseball in 1931. She led her league in home runs that year, and was voted the best woman hockey player in Ontario in 1932. But when arthritis struck again in 1933, she was forced to retire, this time for good. She was just twenty-nine years old.

Bobbie Rosenfeld continued to coach sports for the next few years, and from 1937 to 1957 she wrote a sports column for the *Globe and Mail*. She was inducted into the Canadian Sports Hall of Fame in 1949 and was named Canada's Female Athlete of the Half-Century in 1950. She died in 1969, at the age of sixty-five. To this day, the Canadian Press awards the Bobbie Rosenfeld Trophy to Canada's Female Athlete of the Year.

# Lucien Dumais
## 1905–1993

I
T WAS EARLY MORNING, August 19, 1942. Sergeant Lucien
Dumais, along with 600 other men from Les Fusiliers Mont-
Royal, waited in a flotilla of small boats off the coast of
France. By the time he and the rest of his regiment started to
wade ashore in the third wave of the landing, it was clear that a
disaster was unfolding. The early morning raid on the resort
town of Dieppe was supposed to be a surprise. But the Germans,
who held fortified positions on the cliffs above the town, were
well prepared. They raked the shoreline with bullets and mortar
fire. Men were cut down in such numbers on the stony beach
that their bodies piled up, one on top of the other. As Dumais

waded ashore, he saw that the sea was red with the blood of the dead and wounded, floating in the water.

The raid on Dieppe had been intended as a trial run for a larger-scale Allied invasion of Europe. And lessons were learned that would be put to good use on D-Day in 1944—but at a terrible cost. Of the 6,000 men participating in the Dieppe raid, nearly 5,000 were Canadians. Less than half of them made it back to England: almost 1,000 were killed, and more than 1,800 Canadian troops were taken prisoner by the Germans. Among them was Lucien Dumais. But he would not be a prisoner for long.

Lucien Adélard Dumais was born in Montreal, Quebec. Although there had never been any soldiers in his family, he grew up wanting to be one. Even as a child, he commanded his younger brother and his sisters in war games, although his parents disapproved. He also enjoyed rough contact sports. Dumais admitted much later in life that he always felt he had to be extra tough to make up for his small size. As it turned out, Dumais's scrappiness served him well in the Canadian military. At first he was a part-time volunteer in the army reserve. He drilled on weekends and in the summertime with a proud old French-Canadian infantry regiment, Les Fusiliers Mont-Royal. However, in 1937, recognizing his abilities, his regiment sent him to the Military College at St. Jean.

When the Second World War broke out in 1939, Dumais became a sergeant in the regiment, which was soon shipped to England. It would be almost three years before Canadian troops stationed in Britain would see any combat. In the meantime, Dumais, who was already a champion marksman, was sent on a commando instructors course. Commandos are small groups of soldiers trained for quick, daring raids on the enemy. Dumais liked the challenge of the gruelling course, and the chance, as a commando, to make his own decisions rather than following orders. Before the training was completed, however, his regiment was ordered to take part in the raid on Dieppe.

Dumais was one of a small group of men who fought their way to the casino in Dieppe and captured it from the Germans. However, they were greatly outnumbered and after a few hours had to surrender. The Germans loaded their prisoners into railway cattle cars to take them to a prisoner-of-war camp. However, Dumais and two other men pried the boards off a window and wriggled out. The French Resistance—French people working secretly against the Germans who occupied their country—helped Dumais travel across France to Spain and then to the British base at Gibraltar. From there he was flown to England and safety. But his war was far from over.

The British immediately saw Dumais's value. He was tough, daring, a French speaker—and he had just made a successful journey right across France, so he knew the transportation routes. MI-9—the branch of British intelligence that handled "E and E" (escape and evasion) networks—asked Dumais to return to France. He would be an undercover agent, helping Allied airmen who were downed in combat to escape from France. It was dangerous work. MI-9 explained to Dumais that they would not be able to rescue him or help him in any way once he was in France. If he was captured by the Gestapo—the German secret police—he would be shot. Dumais agreed to return to the country he had risked his life to escape.

Lucien Dumais, now thirty-eight, and a young Canadian radio operator, Raymond LaBrosse, trained together for their mission. They learned parachute jumping, pistol shooting, jiu-jitsu, how to build and operate wireless radio sets, and how to send messages in code. They were given fountain pens that fired tear gas, buttons that hid compasses, and a set of forged documents. Then, with new identities—Lucien Dumais was to be a French mortician named Lucien Desbiens—they were parachuted into a meadow 80 kilometres from Paris one night in November 1943.

Dumais and LaBrosse set up "Operation Bonaparte," which was, in turn, part of a larger escape network called "Shelburne." This was one of the most successful escape networks of the Second World War. The two Canadians could not work alone. They had to set up a network of French people who would risk their lives to help them, and they had to use their own instincts about who could be trusted. They had to find "safe houses" (where Allied airmen could stay), provide clothes and food for the downed flyers, and, often, locate doctors who could treat any injured pilots. Before the airmen could travel in disguise, they had to be taught how to blend in with the French population, even such things as the French labourer's way of holding a cigarette.

The two Canadians also had to find a safe location where they could exchange coded messages with MI-9 in London, without risking interception by the Germans. Eventually they settled on a remote stone farmhouse near the Brittany coast of France. From here, using their radio, they made risky arrangements for Allied airmen to be smuggled out of France by boat. On moonless nights, the escapees would make their way down the steep cliff to the beach. They would briefly shine a flashlight out to sea, hoping that German patrols would not see the signal. Soon, small rubber rafts would appear out of the blackness for the rendezvous that the Canadian agents had pre-arranged. First, the boats would unload vital supplies for Dumais and LaBrosse, including arms and French currency. Then the airmen would be taken aboard and rowed out to a waiting British gunboat that would get them back to England. During the spring of

1944, Dumais and LaBrosse helped more than 120 men escape from France—and they never lost a single one of the men whose escapes they planned. After the Allied invasion of Europe in June 1944, so many rail lines had been destroyed that escaping airmen could no longer make their way to the coast and the safe farmhouse. Lucien Dumais then went to work with the French Resistance, fighting alongside them against the Germans. France was liberated in August 1944, but Dumais stayed on for a few more months, helping to round up German agents. Only then did he return to his family in Canada. After experiencing so much violence and danger, he was ready for a peaceful, civilian life.

# Elizabeth Gregory
# "Elsie" MacGill
## 1905–1980

E LSIE MacGILL WAS NEVER AFRAID to pursue her goals,
even if no woman ever had achieved them before. Her
own mother, Helen Gregory MacGill, was her inspiration.
Helen MacGill was the first woman judge in British Columbia, a
world-travelling journalist, and a crusader for women's rights.
Elsie MacGill's life, too, would be a series of "firsts."

Elizabeth Muriel Gregory MacGill, usually known as Elsie,
was born in Vancouver on March 27, 1905. In 1927 she became
the first woman in Canada to receive a degree in electrical engineering—from the University of Toronto. After graduation she
was hired by the Austin Automobile Company in Michigan. At

first she worked on the design of cars, but when her employer entered the aircraft industry, she became interested in aeronautics, the science of flight. So she returned to school and, in 1929, became the first woman in North America to earn a master's degree in aeronautical engineering, this time from the University of Michigan. By then, MacGill was facing a far greater challenge: in the final weeks of her program, she had been stricken with polio. She insisted on finishing the year, carried by friends to and from her classes. Then she set about making as full a recovery as she could.

While MacGill rested, she wrote articles about aviation and worked on her own airplane designs. When she was strong enough to get around, using a wheelchair or canes, she applied to—and was accepted by—the Massachusetts Institute of Technology for further studies. In 1934, she went to work for Fairchild Aircraft in Longueuil, Quebec, where she helped design the first all-metal aircraft ever built in Canada.

MacGill would have loved to learn to fly, but polio had left her physically unable to pilot a plane. However, she made a point of accompanying the pilot on all test flights of her planes, even the first, most dangerous trials. She felt that the only way to assess the plane's performance was to experience it for herself.

When she was thirty-three, MacGill became chief engineer in the aircraft division of the Canadian Car and Foundry Company in Fort William (later Thunder Bay), Ontario. MacGill was excited to have achieved such an important post so early in her career. She was soon busy designing and then overseeing the testing of the Maple Leaf Trainer—the first aircraft completely designed by a woman. But the greatest challenge of her career was just ahead.

In 1939 Canada went to war against Nazi Germany, fighting alongside Britain and other Allied countries. Canadian Car threw all its resources into manufacturing a fighter plane called the Hawker Hurricane for the British government. The plant was completely revamped, and 4,500 men and women were hired to work on the airplane. MacGill had to manage this large workforce, most of whom had never worked on airplane production before. She was also in charge of the design and manufacture of all the tools and equipment that would be needed to produce the parts of the Hurricane—and it had 60,000 parts.

Between the fall of 1939 and the spring of 1940, Poland, Denmark, Norway, Belgium, Holland, and France fell to the German blitzkrieg (lightning war)—an all-out assault from the air, followed quickly by an overwhelming invasion of ground forces. Britain used these months to build up a stock of planes for an attack on England they knew would come. Most of these aircraft were built in its own factories, but Canada built thousands.

At the end of the summer in 1940, the Battle of Britain was fought in the skies over southeast England. Royal Air Force fighter planes, with crews from Great Britain, Canada, and other Allied countries, battled a much greater number of Luftwaffe (German airforce) invaders. The air battle was planned by Germany as a prelude to an invasion of the British Isles from the sea. But by October, the RAF had still not been defeated, and the Luftwaffe stopped its bombing raids. The invasion never did come, and England was saved.

Several hundred of the Hawker Hurricanes in the Battle of Britain were built in MacGill's plant. By the time it made its last shipment in 1943, Canadian Car had turned out roughly 1,400 Hurricanes. Some of them were "winterized" versions— fitted with skis and de-icing equipment—designed by MacGill.

MacGill received a great deal of attention in newspapers and magazines for her work at Canadian Car. She was even featured in a wartime comic book as "Queen of the Hurricanes"!

However, because she was "a woman in a man's field," as they put it, some articles spent as much time describing her hair, clothes, and interest in cooking as they did describing her engineering achievements. Among engineers, however, her outstanding ability was respected.

In 1943 MacGill married a widower with three children. The family moved to Toronto and she set up her own consulting business. Both government and private industry welcomed her input, and she became recognized as a leading figure in the aeronautics industry.

In 1953 MacGill published a book about Helen Gregory MacGill entitled *My Mother, the Judge*. Like her mother, MacGill was active in the women's movement. In 1967 she was one of the members on the pioneering Royal Commission on the Status of Women. In her reports for the Commission, MacGill argued for workplace equality and tax amendments that would help working mothers to pay for child care. In the years following, MacGill remained active in a number of women's organizations, and she continued to advocate a greater role for women in the professions and in government.

Throughout her career, MacGill received many awards and honours, including the Gzowski medal from the Engineering Institute of Canada, the Award for Meritorious Contribution to Engineering from the Society of Women Engineers (an American organization), and the Amelia Earhart medal from the Ninety-Nines, an organization of women pilots. In 1971 she received the Order of Canada. In 1979, a woman who was establishing an organization for Women in Science and Engineering sought MacGill's support, explaining, "You are the Number One Canadian woman engineer to look up to."

When Elsie MacGill died in November 1980, a memorial service was held for her in Toronto. The program for the service included a passage MacGill had written about her mother, and applied it to her own achievements: "Thus she did what few do—influenced her times for good and left a lasting mark behind her."

# Andrew Mynarski
## 1916–1944

T HE VICTORIA CROSS is the highest medal for bravery
awarded to members of British and Commonwealth
forces. Of the more than 1 million Canadians who
served in the Second World War, only sixteen received the
Victoria Cross. Pilot Officer Andrew Charles Mynarski was
one of them.

Born in Winnipeg, Manitoba, the son of recent immigrants
from Poland, Andrew Mynarski was a quiet, good-natured boy
who enjoyed working with his hands. In the basement workshop
of his house, he spent many after-school hours on his wood-
working projects. He even designed and built furniture.

When his father died, Mynarski had to leave school to help support his mother, two brothers, and three sisters. For four years he worked as a cutter at a Winnipeg furrier. When the Second World War broke out, he joined the Royal Canadian Air Force, and after training in Canada, he went overseas as an air gunner.

In the spring of 1944, the Allies (including the British, Canadians, and Americans) were undertaking an invasion of Europe, where Nazi Germany had occupied many countries, including France. Andrew Mynarski was stationed in England with the 419 Moose Squadron, flying bombing runs over France in a Lancaster. Lancasters were powerful military aircraft, capable of carrying almost their own weight in bombs. They generally flew under cover of darkness, because their only defences against enemy aircraft were a few machine guns, manned by air gunners in swivelling, Plexiglas turrets. The turrets were so cramped that the men in their flight suits could barely squeeze into them. In flight, the temperature in the turrets could drop to −40 degrees Celsius. Mynarski's station was the mid-upper turret, halfway down the plane. His friend Pat Brophy was the rear gunner, at the very tail end of the Lancaster.

On the warm evening of June 12, 1944, Mynarski's crew of seven sprawled on the grass near their plane, waiting for the hour of takeoff. This was to be their thirteenth mission, and by the time they were over their target—the railway yards at Cambrai, France—it would be Friday the thirteenth. The men kidded each other about the bad omen. When Mynarski found a four-leaf clover in the grass, he insisted that Pat Brophy should take it along for good luck. Brophy tucked it into his flight helmet.

Soon after, the Lancaster set off on its mission. Shortly after it crossed the French coastline, it was caught in enemy searchlights. The pilot took some evasive manoeuvres, and soon they were in the safety of darkness again. The crew breathed a sigh of relief. But as the plane began descending to the level for the planned attack, a German fighter plane came in underneath the Lancaster—where it was most vulnerable—and fired. Explosions rocked the aircraft, and both port (left-side) engines began to spurt flames. The hydraulic lines that powered the rear turret were cut, and the fluid leaking from the lines caught fire. The rear of the plane became an inferno.

The pilot, no longer able to control the aircraft, gave the order for all crew to bail out. Mynarski left his post and struggled back to the rear door. Through the flames, he could see Pat Brophy struggling desperately to free himself. The rear turret had jammed in a position where it didn't line up with the door, and Brophy was trapped.

By now, all of the other crew members had made their escapes. But Mynarski, who couldn't bring himself to leave Brophy, crawled through the blazing hydraulic fluid. With his flight suit and parachute in flames, he fought to turn Brophy's turret with a fire axe, and with his bare hands. When Brophy saw that it was hopeless, he urged Mynarski to bail out and save himself. Finally, Mynarski complied. Before jumping, he stood to attention at the escape hatch and saluted Brophy.

French witnesses on the ground saw Mynarski plunging to earth in flames. They ran toward the spot where he landed and carried him to a local doctor. But Andrew Mynarski was so severely injured that he died shortly afterward.

Meanwhile, the unpiloted plane glided down to earth and hit a tree. The aircraft spun around, the rear turret shot open, and Pat Brophy was thrown clear, shaken but barely injured. The other crew members were scattered over a wide area. Some were captured by the Germans and became prisoners of war. It wasn't until the war ended that they met up again, and Brophy could finally tell them what had happened.

In the confusion of battle, many acts of bravery pass unrecorded, because there are no witnesses, or because all the witnesses are killed. Pat Brophy often said that he believed his life had been saved so that he could tell others about Mynarski's courage and self-sacrifice.

Andrew Mynarski is buried in Meharicourt, France. His Victoria Cross is on display at the Air Command Headquarters in his hometown of Winnipeg.

# The Dionne Quintuplets

born 1934

Emilie d. 1954, Marie d. 1970,

Yvonne d. 2001, Annette, Cécile

O N MAY 18, 1934, in the early hours of the morning, five baby girls—identical quintuplets—were born to Elzire and Oliva Dionne. The babies arrived two months prematurely, in the Dionnes' small farmhouse near Corbeil, Ontario, with only Elzire's aunt and a woman neighbour to assist. The Dionnes had little money, and their house had no plumbing or electricity. As the first tiny babies were born, the women wrapped them in blankets and placed them in a basket near the stove for warmth.

Dr. Allan Dafoe, from the nearby town of Callandar, was sent for, and he arrived in time to deliver the last three of the quintuplets. Each baby weighed about two pounds, so small that it could fit in the palm of an adult's hand. Dr. Dafoe did not expect the babies to live because no quintuplets had ever survived before. But the babies—named Annette, Cécile, Yvonne, Marie, and Emilie—did live on. When reporters got hold of the story, the quintuplets became front-page news. The 1930s were the tough years of the Great Depression, when many people were out of work, so the birth of "the miracle babies" was a welcome, cheerful story.

Elzire Dionne could not possibly feed five hungry babies all by herself, so women from surrounding villages brought breast milk for the girls. But the Dionnes worried about the future. They already had five children and could not afford to feed and clothe a family that had doubled overnight. Dr. Dafoe and the parish priest advised Oliva Dionne to accept a $50,000 offer to exhibit his daughters at the Chicago World's Fair. When this was reported in the newspapers, the public was outraged. In the end, Oliva Dionne turned down the money, but the damage was done. The Ontario government then decided that the Dionnes could not be trusted to raise their own daughters.

When the government took over care of the quintuplets, a nine-room nursery was built across the road from the family's farmhouse. Here the quints would live, cared for by a team of doctors and nurses. Every minute of their day was organized, with a rigid schedule for mealtimes, playtimes, and bathtimes. The experts hired to look after the quints were determined to raise them "scientifically." They were measured and studied, and everything they said and did was written down. The nurses were instructed never to spank the girls, but never to hug them, either. Even their own parents had to make an appointment to see them. Cécile said that she learned the word "doctor" before she learned the word "mother."

Tourists flocked to northern Ontario to see the quints. At first, their nurses would bring them out to the nursery balcony to show them to the crowds below. Later, tourists could view the quints three times a day behind screened glass windows. Supposedly the little girls could not see the visitors, but Cécile later said that they saw movement and heard noises and knew they were being watched as they played. The nursery had grown into a complex of buildings called Quintland, with long lineups of visitors waiting to see the girls. The government, which was supposed to protect the girls, instead turned them into an exhibit in a theme park. They were Canada's biggest tourist attraction. About 3 million people visited Quintland between 1934 and 1943, and about $500 million flowed into Ontario's economy. Hotels, restaurants, gas stations, and souvenir stands opened in nearby Callandar and North Bay to serve the stream of visitors.

The quintuplets knew nothing of this; in the first nine years of their lives, Annette, Cécile, Yvonne, Marie, and Émilie hardly ever left the grounds of Quintland. One rare excursion brought them to Toronto at age five to meet the King and Queen, who were on a tour of Canada. Newsreels, which in the days before television were screened in movie theatres, showed five little girls with large, round eyes and curly dark hair tied with bows. They were beautifully dressed in matching outfits, but in most pictures from the Toronto visit, the girls have wistful, unsmiling faces. Cécile Dionne, who in later years became the most outspoken of the quints, asked in 1997, "How come they didn't see how tired we were and how unhappy we were? I can't understand that." But to a public which saw what it wanted and needed to see, the Dionne Quintuplets were living a fairy-tale life—they were rich, famous, and adored.

Hollywood made three movies about the quintuplets. Even Allan Dafoe, the small-town doctor, became an international celebrity, publishing several books about baby and child care. There were Dionne Quintuplet dolls and colouring books. Their faces were used to sell hundreds of products, including canned milk, corn syrup, baby clothes, shampoo, and even typewriters. There should have been more than enough money to keep the quintuplets financially secure for the rest of their lives. But it didn't turn out that way.

All the time the quintuplets were living at Quintland, Elzire and Oliva Dionne waged a desperate legal battle to get their daughters back. After eight years, the parents were successful, and the five girls moved into a new, large house (built with the quints' earnings) with their family. But it was too late. The quints and their parents and brothers and sisters were strangers to one another, with suspicion and resentment on both sides.

When they were eighteen years old, the girls left home to study at a convent in Nicolet, Quebec, and from then on had almost no contact with their parents. They moved to Montreal, to try to live the private lives they had never had. About $1 million— a fraction of the money they had earned—had actually ended up in a trust fund for the girls. They were to receive this money when they turned twenty-one, in 1955. By then, they were four: Emilie had died during an epileptic seizure in 1954. When the remaining Dionne sisters began to receive payments from their trust fund money, they found that instead of growing since the years when they were children, the fund had actually shrunk to about $800,000.

Adult life was difficult for the sisters, so close to each other, and so strangely raised without contact with other people. Marie, Annette, and Cécile married and had children—two for Marie, three for Annette, and five for Cécile—but all the

marriages ended unhappily. Divorce settlements, bad investments, and other misfortunes ate away at the money. Marie died
in 1970, and the remaining three sisters carried on, living simple
lives on what little remained of their trust fund.

Then, in the early 1990s, Annette, Cécile, and Yvonne decided
to fight back. They published a book about the way they had
been treated at the government-run Quintland, which they
described as "inhuman." And they demanded that the government account for all the money they had earned as children.
They had learned, for instance, that all the expenses of running
their childhood nursery had been deducted from their earnings.

In February 1998, Premier Mike Harris of Ontario
announced that each of the women would receive $2,000 per
month, tax-free. But there would be no inquiry about the government's handling of the Dionnes' money, and no apology. The
citizens of Ontario were deeply dissatisfied with the government's stand. In letters to the editor, calls to radio talk shows,
and complaints to their members of Parliament, they made it
clear that they thought the Dionne sisters had been treated
shamefully. The sisters themselves—three shy and quiet women
now in their sixties—appeared at a televised press conference to
say that they wanted justice, not charity. As Cécile explained,
they were asking for "only what was taken from us, what was
stolen from our trust fund."

The government quickly gave in. The Dionne sisters were to
receive $4 million, tax-free, from the government. In addition,
Premier Harris travelled to their home in St. Bruno, Quebec, to
apologize personally for the way the government had handled
their affairs during the first nine years of their lives. Yvonne
died in 2001, with the peace of mind that came from having
received justice at last. Annette and Cécile have returned to the
quiet lives they prefer.

# Photo Credits

p. 1 Donald Smith, Lord Strathcona: National Archives of Canada, C-17399.

p. 7 Sandford Fleming: National Archives of Canada, C-014126.

p. 13 Timothy Eaton: Timothy Eaton. Founder T. Eaton Company Limited 1869. Archives of Ontario.

p. 18 Hannah Maynard: Hannah Maynard self-portrait trick photograph (multiple images) ca. 1893-1867. Courtesy of BC Archives. Call Number: F-02852.

p. 23 Anderson Ruffin Abbott: Courtesy of the Ontario Black History Society.

p. 28 Wilfrid Laurier: National Archives of Canada, C-016741.

p. 34 Henri Bourassa: National Archives of Canada, C-27360.

p. 40 John Ware: Glenbow Archives, Calgary. (NA-263-1) The John Ware Family.

p. 44 Alexander Graham Bell: The New Brunswick Museum, Saint John, N.B.

p. 49 Sam Steele: RCMP Museum, Regina, Saskatchewan.

p. 55 Joseph-Elzéar Bernier: The New Brunswick Museum, Saint John, N.B.

p. 60 Robert Borden: National Archives of Canada, 17946.

p. 66 Ned Hanlan: National Archives of Canada, PA-135260. Photographer: D.C. Ferguson.

p. 71 Kit Coleman: National Archives of Canada, PA-164917. Photographer: R. Kennedy.

p. 75 Adelaide Hunter Hoodless: National Archives of Canada, PA-203295.

p. 79 Joseph Burr Tyrrell: The Thomas Fisher Rare Book Library, University of Toronto.

p. 84 E. Cora Hind: Provincial Archives of Manitoba, N978.

p. 89 E. Pauline Johnson: National Archives of Canada, C-85125.

p. 94 James Naismith: University Archives, Kenneth Spencer Research Library, University of Kansas Libraries.

p. 99 Martha Black: National Archives of Canada, C-23354. Photographer Pierre Brunet.

p. 103 Reginald Fessenden: North Carolina Department of History and Archives.

p. 108 Maude Abbott: National Archives of Canada, C-9479.

p. 114 Stephen Leacock: National Archives of Canada. United Church of Canada Collection, PA-110154

p. 119 R.B. Bennett: National Archives of Canada, C-7731.

**p. 125** Emily Carr: Courtesy J. Ross Robertson Collection, Metropolitan Toronto Library.

**p. 131** Sam McLaughlin: Col. R.S. (Sam) McLaughlin. Photo by Cavouk. Archival Holdings at Parkwood, The R.S. McLaughlin Estate.

**p. 136** Nellie McClung: National Archives of Canada, PA-030212.

**p. 142** William Lyon Mackenzie King: National Archives of Canada, C-000387.

**p. 150** Lucy Maud Montgomery: Public Archives and Records, Office of Prince Edward Island. Acc.#311011.

**p. 155** Tom Thomson: National Archives of Canada, C-17399.

**p. 160** Arthur Currie: National Archives of Canada, PA-001370.

**p. 166** John McCrae: Courtesy of Guelph Museums—McCrae House Collection.

**p. 171** Billy Bishop: National Archives of Canada, PA-001654. Photographer: William Rider-Rider.

**p. 176** J.S. Woodsworth: National Archives of Canada, C-003940.

**p. 182** Robert Boyd Russell: Provincial Archives of Manitoba. Robert Boyd Russell, N10134.

**p. 189** Angus Walters: Angus Walters at the wheel of schooner *Bluenose*. From the collection of the Maritime Museum of the Atlantic, Halifax, Nova Scotia, Canada.

**p. 195** Lester and Frank Patrick: Canada's Sports Hall of Fame.

**p. 200** Tom Longboat: National Archives of Canada, C-014090. Photographer: Charles Aylette.

**p. 206** Archibald Stansfeld Belaney ("Grey Owl"): Archives of Ontario.

**p. 212** Norman Bethune: Artist Irma Coucill. Used with the permission of the Canadian Medical Hall of Fame, London, Ontario.

**p. 218** Agnes Macphail: National Archives of Canada, C-006908.

**p. 223** Frederick Banting: National Archives of Canada, PA-123481.

**p. 228** Wilfrid Reid "Wop" May: National Archives of Canada, C-057591.

**p. 233** Lionel Conacher: Canada's Sports Hall of Fame.

**p. 238** Howie Morenz: CP Picture Archive.

**p. 243** Bobbie Rosenfeld: Canada's Sports Hall of Fame.

**p. 248** Lucien Dumais: Photo from: http://membres.lycos.fr/francelibre/lucien.htm

**p. 253** Elizabeth Gregory "Elsie" MacGill: National Archives of Canada, PA-148464. Photographer: Ashley & Crippen.

**p. 258** Andrew Mynarski: National Archives of Canada. PA-020826. Painted by Paul Goranson in 1947.

**p. 262** Dionne Quintuplets: Dionne Quints Museum Collection with expressed permission of Annette and Cécile Dionne.

# Index

Abbott, Anderson Ruffin 23–27
Abbott, Maude 108–113
Aberdeen, Lady 77–78
Addams, Jane 143
Aitkin, Max (Lord Beaverbrook) 120
Alaska Boundary Dispute 36, 52
Albertosaurus 80
Algonquin Park 155, 158
Allan, Hugh 4
Anahareo. *See* Bernard, Gertrude
*Anne of Green Gables* (Montgomery) 150, 152
anti-Conscription riots 33, 38
Arctic 55, 56–58

Bank of Canada 123
Banting, Frederick 214, 223–227
Barker, William 174
baseball 235–236, 239, 243, 247
basketball
    invention of 96–97
    rules of 97
Basketball Hall of Fame 98
Battle of Britain 255
Belaney, Archibald Stansfeld ("Grey Owl") 206–211
Bell, Alexander Graham 44–48, 103
Bell, Jane 246
Bennett, R.B. 119–124, 147
"Bennett Buggies" 122
Bernard, Gertrude 208–210
Bernier, Joseph-Elzéar 55–59
Best, Charles 226–227
Bethune, Norman 212–217
Bishop, William Avery "Billy" 171–175
Black, Martha Louise 99–102
*Bluenose* (schooner) 189–194
*Bluenose II* (schooner) 194
Bobbie Rosenfeld Trophy 247
Boer War 6, 31–32, 36, 53, 156, 168, 233
*Book of Small, The* (Carr) 130
Borden, Robert 33, 37, 60–65, 121

Boston Marathon 201, 203
Boucher, Billy 241
Bourassa, Henri 32, 34–39
British Commonwealth Air Training Plan 232
British Empire 6, 12, 31, 37, 62, 63, 167, 232, 233
Brophy, Pat 259–261
Brown, Roy 230–231
Buick Motor Company 133–134
Byng, Julian 146, 161, 164

Canadian Aviation Hall of Fame 232
Canadian Broadcasting Corporation (CBC) 141
Canadian Car and Foundry Company 254–255
Canadian National Exhibition 70
Canadian Pacific Railway 4–5, 10–11, 51–52, 121, 183, 195
Canadian Sports Hall of Fame 237, 247
Canadian Wheat Board 123
Canadian Women's Press Club 74
Capilano, Chief Joe 92
Carr, Emily 125–130
Catherwood, Ethel 246
cattle drives 41–42
Chicago Blackhawks (hockey team) 242
Chicago World's Fair (1933 and 1934) 192, 263
Chilkoot Pass 100
China, at war with Japan 216–217
Churchill, Winston 62–63
Civil War, American 23–26, 40
Civil War, Spanish 215–216
Coleman, Kit 71–74
Collip, James 226
Columbian Exposition (Chicago, 1893) 73, 104
Communist Party 215
Conacher, Charlie 235, 236
Conacher, Lionel 233–237

Conscription
First World War 33, 38, 64, 145, 179, 220
Second World War 39, 147–148
Conservative Party 4, 37, 61–62, 64–65,
120–121, 145–148, 180
Co-operative Commonwealth Federation
(CCF) 148, 181, 222
Cook, Myrtle 246
Country Life (British magazine) 209
cowboys 40–43
CPR. See Canadian Pacific Railway
Currie, Arthur 160–165
Curtiss, Glenn 47

Dafoe, Allan 263, 265
Dafoe, John Wesley 88
Depression. See Great Depression
Dickins, "Punch" 232
Dieppe Raid 248–249
Dionne, Elzire 262, 263, 265
Dionne, Oliva 262, 263, 265
Dionne Quintuplets 262–266
Distinguished Flying Cross 171, 231
domestic science 76–77
Dominion Parks Service 209
Dumais, Lucien 248–252
Duplessis, Maurice 39

Eaton, John Craig 17
Eaton, Timothy 13–17
Eaton's (store) 15–17
Edison, Thomas Alva 103–104
Edmonton Eskimos 235
Edward VII (King) 10, 12
Edwards, Henrietta Muir 140
Elements of Political Science (Leacock) 116
Elizabeth II (Queen) 206
Emily trilogy (Montgomery) 153

Family Allowance Act 148
Federated Labour Party 179
Federation of Medical Women of Canada
113
Fenians 50
Fessenden, Reginald 103–107
First World War 33, 38–39, 53, 63–65,
140, 145, 158, 160–161, 163–165,
166–167, 168–170, 172–174, 179, 184,

204, 208, 213–214, 219–220, 224–225,
230–231
Fleming, Sandford 5, 7–12
Flint and Feather (Johnson) 92
football 234–235, 237
Ford Motor Company 133
Free Trade 33. See also Reciprocity
French Resistance (Second World War)
250–252
Frontier College 213

General Motors of Canada 134–135
Geological Survey of Canada 81–82
George V (King) 53, 58, 63, 164, 171, 193,
226, 231
"Gertrude the Governess" (Leacock) 116
gold rush
Fraser River 19
Klondike 52–53, 82, 99–100
Yellowknife 82
Governor General's Award for Literature
117, 129
Great Depression 122–123, 180, 193, 205, 237
Grey, Lord 168
Grey Cup 234–235
Grey Owl. See Belaney, Archibald Stansfeld
Group of Seven 129, 159, 227
Growing Pains (Carr) 130

Hanlan, Ned 66–70
Harris, Lawren 129, 158, 159
Harris, Mike 266
Hart Trophy 241
Hawker Hurricane (airplane) 255
Helmer, Alexis 169
Hind, E. Cora 84–88, 137
hockey 195–199, 234–237, 238–242, 243–244
rules of 196, 197, 199
Hockey Hall of Fame 199, 237, 242
Hoodless, Adelaide Hunter 75–78
Horner, Vic 229
House of All Sorts, The (Carr) 130
Hudson's Bay Company 2–4, 168
Hughes, Sam 163, 165
hydrofoils 48

Imperial War Cabinet 63
"In Flanders Fields" 166, 169

Independent Labour Party 180
Industrial Disputes Investigation Act 144
Industrial Workers of the World (the "Wobblies") 184
*Industry and Humanity* (King) 145
insulin, discovery of 223–224, 225–226
International Association of Machinists (IAM) 183, 185
Inuit 58
Irish Potato Famine 13–14

*Jack Pine, The* (Thomson) 159
Jackson, A.Y. 158, 159, 227
Jelly Roll and Rawhide (beavers) 209, 210
Johnson, E. Pauline 89–93, 201
Johnston, Frank 159
Joliat, Aurel 241

Keller, Helen 46
King, William Lyon Mackenzie 142–149, 180
Kirkland Lake Gold Mining Company 82, 83
*Klee Wyck* (Carr) 129
Klondike, 52

LaBrosse, Raymond 250–252
Lancaster (airplane) 259–260
labour unions 16, 179–180, 182–188
Last Spike, the 1, 5, 11, 52
Laurier, Wilfrid 28–33, 35–39, 55–56, 61–62, 73, 143
Lavergne, Emilie 29
Leacock, Stephen 114–118
League of Nations 65
*Legends of Vancouver* (Johnson) 93
Liberal Party 30–33, 35–38, 144–148, 180, 237
Lincoln, Abraham 26, 40
Lipton Cup (race) 192
*Literary Lapses* (Leacock) 116
Longboat, Tom 200–205
Luckock, Rae 222

MacDonald, J.E.H. 157, 158, 159
Macdonald, Hugh John 86
Macdonald, John A. 4,5, 30
MacGill, Elizabeth Gregory "Elsie" 253–257
MacGill, Helen Gregory 253, 255, 257

Mackenzie, Alexander (prime minister) 5
Mackenzie, William Lyon 143
Mackenzie King. *See* King, William Lyon Mackenzie
Mackenzie-Papineau Battalion 215
*Maclean's* (magazine) 237
Macleod, J.R.R. 226–227
Macphail, Agnes 102, 218–232
"Mad Trapper," the 232
Manitoba Schools Question 30–31, 37
Maple Leaf Trainer (airplane) 254
March on Ottawa 123
Marconi, Guglielmo 104–105
May, Court 230, 231
May, Wilfrid Reid "Wop" 228–232
Maynard, Hannah 18–22
McCallum, James 158
McClung, Annie 137–138
McClung, Nellie 136–141
McCrae, John 166–170
McCurdy, J.A.D. 47–48
McGinnis and McGinty (beavers) 208, 209
McKinney, Louise 140
McLaughlin, Sam 131–135
McLaughlin Carriage Works 131–133
McNaughton, Andrew 123
McRaye, Walter 92
Meighen, Arthur 121, 145, 146
*Men of the Last Frontier* (Grey Owl) 209
Métis 30, 35, 50–51
MI-9 (British Intelligence) 250, 251
Military Cross 171, 225
military units, Canadian
    7th Canadian Mounted Rifles 172
    50th Regiment, Gordon Highlanders 163
    419 Moose Squadron 259
    Les Fusiliers Mont-Royal 248, 249
    Lord Strathcona's Horse 53
    Mississauga Horse 172
    Queen's Own Rifles 168
    Royal Canadian Artillery 168
    Royal 22nd ("Van-Doos") 38
    Yukon Infantry 101
Mohawk 89, 90, 91
Mons, attack on 164
Montgomery, Lucy Maud 150–154
Montreal Canadiens (hockey team) 240–242
Montreal Maroons (hockey team) 236

Montreal Wanderers (hockey team) 196
Morenz, Howie 238–242
Morse Code 46, 105, 106
Mulock, William 143
Murphy, Emily 140
"My Financial Career" (Leacock) 116
My Mother, the Judge (MacGill) 256
My Neighbour (Woodsworth) 179
My Seventy Years (Black) 102
Mynarski, Andrew 258–261

Naismith, James 94–98
National Archives of Canada 222
National Council of Women 78
National Gallery of Canada 129, 159
National Hockey Association (NHA) 197
National Hockey League (NHL) 197–199,
   235, 236–237, 240–242
Navy, Royal (Britain) 32, 37, 62–63, 214
Navy, Canadian 62–63
New Democratic Party (NDP). See
   Co-operative Commonwealth Federation
   (CCF)
New York Rangers (hockey team) 198–199,
   242
newspapers, Canadian
   Brantford Expositor 90
   Daily Mail (Toronto) 72
   Dawson News 101
   Défricheur, Le 29–30
   Devoir, Le (Montreal) 37, 38, 39
   Gazette (Montreal) 110, 240
   Globe (Toronto) 15
   Globe and Mail (Toronto) 222, 247
   Herald (Halifax) 191
   Mail and Empire (Toronto) 73–74
   North Bay Nugget 210
   Winnipeg Free Press 83, 86, 137
   Whitehorse Star 102
Nobel Prize for Medicine 226
Nonsense Novels (Leacock) 116
North Pole 56–57
North-West Mounted Police 6, 51–53, 186.
   See also Royal North-West Mounted
   Police
Northern Lake, A (Thomson) 157
Nuu-chah-nulth 126, 129

Ojibwa 207
old age pension 146, 180
Olympic Games
   1896 (Athens) 200
   1904 (St. Louis) 97
   1908 (London) 203
   1928 (Amsterdam) 243, 246
   1936 (Berlin) 98
One Big Union (OBU) 184, 187
Onondaga 201
Order of Canada 135, 256
Order of the British Empire 232
Osler, William 111–112, 167, 168
Ottawa Senators (hockey team) 241

Papineau, Louis-Joseph 34, 35
Parlby, Irene 140
Pacific cable 11–12
Pacific Coast Hockey Association (PCHA)
   197–198, 241
Paris Peace Conference 65
Parliament of Women, The (McClung) 139
Patrick, Craig 199
Patrick, Frank 196–199
Patrick, Lester 195–199
Patrick, Lynn 199
Patrick, Murray ("Muzz") 199
Peary, Robert E. 57
"Persons" Case 140
photography 18–22
Pierce-Arrow (automobile) 133
Prince Albert National Park (Saskatchewan)
   210
Progressive Party 146, 219–220
Punch (British magazine) 169

Quintland 264–265

racism 24–25, 27, 181, 201
radio, invention of 104–106
railways. See also Canadian Pacific Railway
   Grand Trunk Railway 239
   Intercolonial Railway 10
   Ontario, Simcoe and Huron Railway
      9, 10
   St. Paul and Pacific Railway 5
   Timiskaming and Northern Ontario
      Railway 207

ranches
Bar U Ranch 41
Quorn Ranch 41–42
Rebellion of 1837 29, 34
Reciprocity 33, 37, 62
regiments. See Military units
Remembrance Day 16
Renfrew Millionaires (hockey team) 197
Resolution IX 63
"Riders of the Plains" (Johnson) 92
Riding Mountain National Park (Manitoba) 209
Riel, Louis 30, 35, 50
Roblin, Rodmond 139
Roosevelt, Franklin Delano 123
Rosenfeld, Bobbie 243–247
Royal Air Force (RAF) 255
Royal Canadian Air Force (RCAF) 174, 259
Royal Canadian Army Medical Corps 213, 224
Royal Canadian Mounted Police (RCMP) 252
Royal Flying Corps 173, 230–231
Royal North-West Mounted Police 57
Royal Society of Arts and Letters 154
Royal Tyrrell Museum of Paleontology 80
Russell, Robert Boyd 182–188

Saturday Night (magazine) 72, 91
Seattle Metropolitans (hockey team) 198
Second World War 147–148, 174, 222, 232, 237, 249–252, 254–255, 258, 259–260
Sifton, Clifford 32, 36
Silver Dart (airplane) 47
Simpson, George 2–3
Simpson, Robert 15
Six Nations Reserve 89, 201, 204, 205
slavery 23–24, 40
Smith, Donald 1–6, 52
Smith, Ethel 246
Socialist Party 187
sonar 106
"Song My Paddle Sings, The" (Johnson) 91
Sowing Seeds in Danny (McClung) 138
Squamish 92
Spanish-American War 73
standard time, invention of 7–8, 11
Stanley Cup 196, 198, 199, 236, 241, 242

Stanley Park 93
Steele, Sam 6, 49–54
steer-wrestling 42
Stephen, George 4, 5
Stephen Leacock Medal for Humour 118
Strathcona, Lord. See Smith, Donald
Strangers at Our Gates (Woodsworth) 179
suffrage. See women's rights
Sunshine Sketches of a Little Town 116

Tekahionwake. See Johnson, E. Pauline
telegraph 46
telephone, invention of 46, 103
Thompson, Jean 246–247
Thomson, Tom 155–159
Toronto Argonauts (football team) 234
Toronto Maitlands (lacrosse team) 235
Toronto Maple Leafs (baseball team) 236
Toronto Maple Leafs (hockey team) 235, 240
Toronto St. Patricks (hockey team) 235, 240. See also Toronto Maple Leafs (hockey team)
Three-Penny Beaver (Canada's first postage stamp) 9
trade unions. See labour unions
"Train Dogs" 92
Treaty of Versailles 65
Triple-A International League (baseball) 236
Tupper, Charles 61
Tupper, Charles Hibbert 61
Twain, Mark 152
Tyrrell, Joseph Burr 79–83

unemployment insurance 146, 180
Union government 33, 38, 64, 145
Union Nationale 39
United Farmers of Ontario 220
United Nations 175

Van Horne, William Cornelius 5
Vancouver Millionaires (hockey team) 198
Varley, Frederick 157, 158, 159
Victoria (Queen) 6, 31, 73, 233
Victoria Cougars (hockey team) 198, 241
Victoria Cross 171, 174, 258, 261
Victorian Order of Nurses (VON) 77–78
Vimy Ridge, Battle of 64, 160–161, 173
"Visible Speech" 45, 47

Von Richthofen, Manfred (the "Red Baron")
   174, 231
Walters, Angus 189–194
*War Canoes* (Carr) 130
Ware, John 40–43
Western Canada Hockey League 241
Weston Shops (CPR) 183
*White Wampum, The* (Johnson) 91
*Winged Peace* (Bishop) 175
*Winged Warfare* (Bishop) 173
Winnipeg General Strike 145, 179–180,
   185–187
Women's Christian Temperance Union
   (WCTU) 138
Women in Science and Engineering 256

Women's Institutes 77
"Women's Kingdom" (newspaper column)
   72–74
women's rights
   discrimination against women 74, 86,
      109–110, 111–112, 221
   voting rights 64, 87,138–140, 219
Woodsworth, J.S. 176–181, 187
World War I. *See* First World War
World War II. *See* Second World War

Young Men's Christian Association (YMCA)
   96, 98, 202, 203
Young Women's Christian Association
   (YWCA) 96, 202, 203
Ypres, Battle of 163–164, 167, 214